TAKAMIYAMA

The World of Sumo

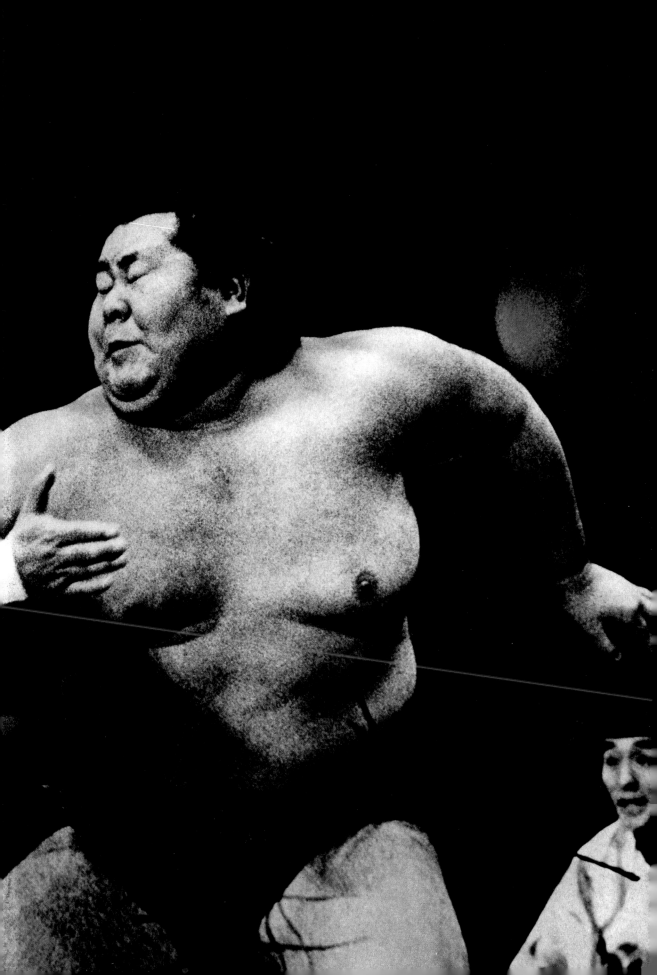

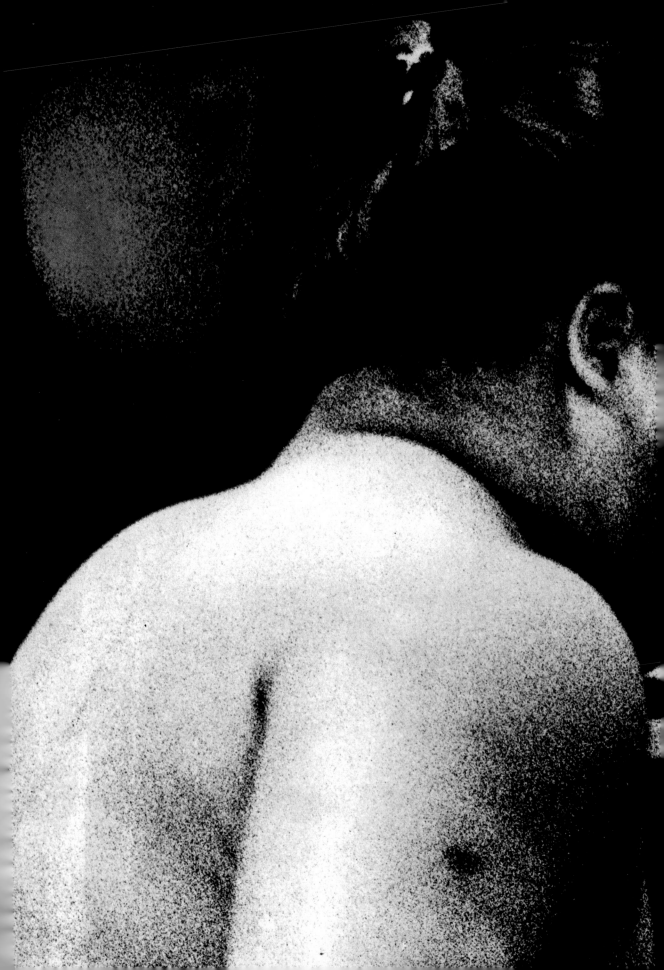

Jesse Kuhaulua
(Daigoro Takamiyama)

with
John Wheeler

photographs by
D. Turner Givens

TAKAMIYAMA

The World of Sumo

Kodansha International

Distributors:

UNITED STATES: Harper & Row, Publishers, Inc.
10 East 53rd street, New York, New York 10022

CANADA: Fitzhenry & Whiteside Limited
150 Lesmill Road, Don Mills, Ontario

CENTRAL AND SOUTH AMERICA: Feffer & Simons Inc.
31 Union Square, New York, New York 10003

BRITISH COMMONWEALTH (excluding Canada and the Far East):
TABS, 51 Weymouth Street, London W.I.

EUROPE: Boxerbooks Inc. Limmatstrasse 111,
8031 Zurich, Switzerland

THAILAND: Central Department Store Ltd.
306 Silom Road, Bangkok

HONG KONG: Books for Asia Ltd.
379 Prince Edward Road, Kowloon

THE FAR EAST: Japan Publication Trading Company
P.O. Box 5030, Tokyo International, Tokyo

JAPAN: Kodansha International Ltd.
2-12-21 Otowa, Bunkyo-ku, Tokyo

Published by Kodansha International Ltd., 2-12-21 Otowa, Bunkyo-ku, Tokyo 112,
Japan, and Kodansha International/USA Ltd., Harper & Row Bldg, 10 East 53rd
Street, New York, New York 10022, and 505 Wells Fargo Bldg, 44 Montgomery
Street, San Francisco, California 94104.

LCC 72-96129
ISBN 0-87011-195-7
JBC 0075-783860-2361

First edition, 1973

Contents

To the people of Hawaii

Acknowledgments

In researching the intricacies of *sumodo* we have had enormous encouragement and assistance from many people and numerous organizations. We would like to mention, in particular, Etsuro Saito and the staff at the Sumo Museum in Kokugikan, who have been extraordinarily patient, Masao Ikeda of *Baseball Magazine* for his advice and for supplying some of the photographs of Jesse's early career and his victories at Nagoya, and the cooperation of the Sumo Association.

We would also like to take this opportunity of acknowleging our sources for some of the early historical information: *Nihongi* [The chronicles of Japan], translated by W. G. Aston, and published by Allen and Unwin, London, and *Kojiki* [Records of ancient matters], translated by Donald Philippi, and published by University of Tokyo Press. *Sumo hyakunenshi* [100 years of sumo], published by Kodansha, Tokyo, was an invaluable source for much of sumo's recent history; and thanks are due to them for permitting us to use the diagrams showing the various sumo throws, and for the prints illustrating a part of sumo's history.

D. Turner Givens, the photographer, would like to extend his appreciation to Kodak (Far East) laboratories for their assistance in processing his material.

Finally, we would like to say a special thank you to all the wrestlers and *oyakata* at Takasago-beya without whose help this book would not have been possible.

Preface

On January 28, 1972, Jesse Kuhaulua became the first recepient of an award for intercultural activity given by the University of Hawaii's East-West Center. The honor is now bestowed annually on the "individual who has made, in everyday life, a significant contribution to the fostering in Asia, the Pacific area and the United States of better relations between the people of the culture in which the individual is working and the people of another culture or cultures." In presenting the award, Chancellor Everett Kleinjans expressed what people on both sides of the Pacific, from coaches, fellow wrestlers, and sumo officials to his countless friends and supporters, have come to feel about the wrestler called Takamiyama: "sumo is much more than a sport—its arts, rituals, and philosophy are imbedded in some 2,000 years of Japanese culture and history. To immerse himself in this culture, and to be accepted with respect and admiration by the Japanese people as Jesse Kuhaulua has been, requires an unusual degree of sensitivity, dedication and a sense of common humanity which transcends cultural barriers."

Hawaii's Jesse Kuhaulua, Japan's Daigoro Takamiyama. More than his exploits in the ring, it is his human achievement, his "heart" as his friend and stablemate Asaarashi would put it, that has earned "Jesse Takamiyama" such esteem and affection. Although an American citizen. Jesse is, in essence, a citizen of two cultures and has become quite unconsciously that rarest kind of cultural ambassador, one whose very existence promotes goodwill between peoples quite apart from governmental or organizational interests.

If Takamiyama "represents" anything other than himself, it is sumo, which has forged his unique identity and projected him into the public eye. His choice of occupations was an unusual one for an American, and he has suffered and triumphed in a world that, by his own admission, may, perhaps, not be entered again by a non-Japanese. More than an autobiography, this book is about that world.

John Wheeler

Tokyo, January 1973

Prologue

Last night we had a helluva typhoon. The storm which violently shook the old buildings of the temple compound where the wrestlers from our stable are staying during the Nagoya tournament has left the city fresh-washed, clean. The cloudless sky glistens an unreal blue, and the air for a rare moment remains pollution-free. But the sultry midsummer humidity has returned making even the early morning hours uncomfortable.

I rise unrefreshed. It was not only the typhoon's clamor that made sleep difficult; it's the pressure. And last night was no different from the past three. Only three days, but it seems like forever. Sure, every tournament seems long: wrestling fifteen days in a row always takes it out of you. But this time everything is different, because I am leading by one precious victory. A win today, the last, means that the dream comes true—my first championship! During the last three days I have begun to believe what I didn't allow myself to imagine two weeks ago. A championship! I can almost taste it.

My mind races ahead to the bout this afternoon: Asahikuni, my opponent, the last hurdle. He is small, about half my size, but agile. He'll probably try to sidestep my charge to get me off balance, or try to trip me. I've got to be careful.

I pass through the vast Buddha hall where the stable's younger, lower-ranked wrestlers bed down. They have been up for hours to have their turn in the practice area and to prepare the day's first meal. Their bedding is stacked neatly to one side, leaving the long rows of tatami mats free to absorb the diagonal rays of sunlight pouring in through the open windows. I glance, and unconsciously nod, toward the altar, but the statues there are veiled in darkness, the sun still too low to penetrate their chamber. Outside, the other upper-ranked wrestlers loll on the porch. I am the last one up today.

"Morning Jesse. Looks like the weatherman's on your side." One of my stablemates touches on the topic on everyone's mind.

"Morning. Sure is quite a day," I reply, dropping down beside him.

There is a consciously thoughtful silence.

Another wrestler breaks the ice.

"Who's today? Asahikuni?"

"Yeah."

"He's little, but tough. Don't go after him too hard and give him the chance to jump aside and trip you. Dig in and let him come to you."

"Yeah." The other wrestlers nod their heads, and the topic quickly changes to the finer points of a golf swing. Soon, a few of the younger wrestlers appear to help us wind our *mawashi* around our middles. Practice will be light, as it is every day of a tournament. We must conserve our energy for the bouts in the afternoon. We move off to the nearby practice area. A wrestler calls out over his shoulder, "Just fight your fight, man. No sweat. And good luck."

"Thanks."

In the training area I go through limbering-up exercises, and then get into the dirt ring against a succession of young, low-ranked stablemates. Just a light work-out—I let my much lighter opponents try to push me out of the circle. I am thinking of Takanohana, the man only one victory behind me in the tournament. He is one of the only two guys who has beaten me this time and always a tough opponent. Should he win today and I lose, it will mean identical 12–3 records and force a playoff between us. Got to avoid that. Got to win it going away by taking Asahikuni. I am dimly aware of the persistent thrusts of the small body against my chest, struggling to push my great bulk backwards. For a moment he becomes Asahikuni. I grab his belt and, with a quick arm throw, send him crashing into the dirt. He jumps up quickly, ready for more. Perhaps someday he'll be a grand champion with many victories under his belt. But today he's just a teenage recruit with big dreams.

Finishing the workout, I pick up a towel and head for the bath. The stable boss has been watching me in the ring silently; he comes over.

"Just one more, Jesse. Bring home the bacon."

The minutes drag as I sit silently in the dressing room, waiting my turn to fight. Wrestlers come and go but no one approaches. They know what I'm going through—many have been here before me. Slowly, so slowly, the bouts proceed. Only one thing matters now: Asahikuni.

The room is already beginning to fill with reporters, as one of my assistants leans over to whisper, "It's time." At last. I check the heavy silk mawashi one final time and then lumber past the restless crowd of newsmen and out towards the arena. Those guys will be all over me in a few minutes if I come back a winner.

I enter the arena and sit down on my cushion beside the raised dirt ring to await my fight. I can feel the quickening anticipation of the capacity crowd. They are as impatient as I am. But there's a difference. Most of them want the drama of a playoff between me and Takanohana. Not that they're rooting for me to lose against Asahikuni. They'd just naturally love the added excitement of a sudden-death fight. Well, this is one time I'm going to have to disappoint them. No play-off today. I'm going to finish it right here.

Takamiyama pushes out Asahikuni on the last day of the 1972 Nagoya Tournament—and ensures himself of the championship. (Baseball Magazine)

Asahikuni sits across the ring from me. He seems nervous, tight. With butterflies in my stomach I'm not exactly calm myself, but I try to look unconcerned. I flash him a quick contemptuous glance, fold my arms and gaze up at the lights. The seconds inch by.

Finally, we face each other. We go stoically through the warming-up rituals, the tension mounting. The referee gives the signal. This is it. I crouch low, but do not charge. He crashes into me and I absorb the impact. No sidestepping, no tripping, he comes at me with all he's got. Grabbing his belt with both hands, I force my weight against him and carefully, relentlessly, I push him back. Suddenly I feel his hand trying to pull me off the belt. I hold fast. Then he tries to twist me off balance with a sharp arm throw. I counter, crouching lower, and keep pushing back. We're at the straw ridge. One more good push and he's out. Careful, Jesse, careful, don't let him twist aside. I thrust forward. His heels jam against the raised boundary and he resists mightily. A little more pressure—I feel him give. That's it! His foot's out. It's over. I did it. I am the champ!

Back in the dressing room. Bedlam. Volleys of flashbulbs and the crush of reporters. Can this all really be happening to me? I feel half-dazed and almost giddy. My eyes moisten. I guess it's okay to let a few tears fall now. It was tough holding them back in the arena right after the bout was over. Wiping my eyes dry, I feel the small bandage covering the gash I received in a head-butting encounter with my opponent yesterday. But the pain is gone. I try to make sense out of the whole thing, try to get used to an entirely new role, but I am soon engulfed by the newspapermen and their barrage of questions.

"Can you describe your feelings at this moment in one word?"

"Joy. The greatest. Simply that."

"What did you think at the moment you won your last bout today, the one that decided the championship?"

"I made it. It's like a dream."

"What do you remember about the fight itself?"

"Absolutely nothing. I was in a trance once the bout started. I remember thinking as we got in the ring that I'd have to watch him closely at the charge and be real careful. I was tight, and my heart was pounding."

"Are those tears?"

"No, it's sweat."

"What do you most want to do now?"

"Rest. These last three days seemed like a month. But if I were born again, I'd become a sumo wrestler. This makes it all worth it."

The questions continue. I try to answer clearly but it becomes hard to think. Fortunately I am soon rescued by a fellow wrestler who breaks through the wall of reporters to tell me the last bout of the day is over. They are ready for the awards ceremony.

"Takamiyama!" "Takamiyama!" "Jesse!" "Takamiyama!" I enter the arena for the second time today. Shouts of my Japanese and American names rise

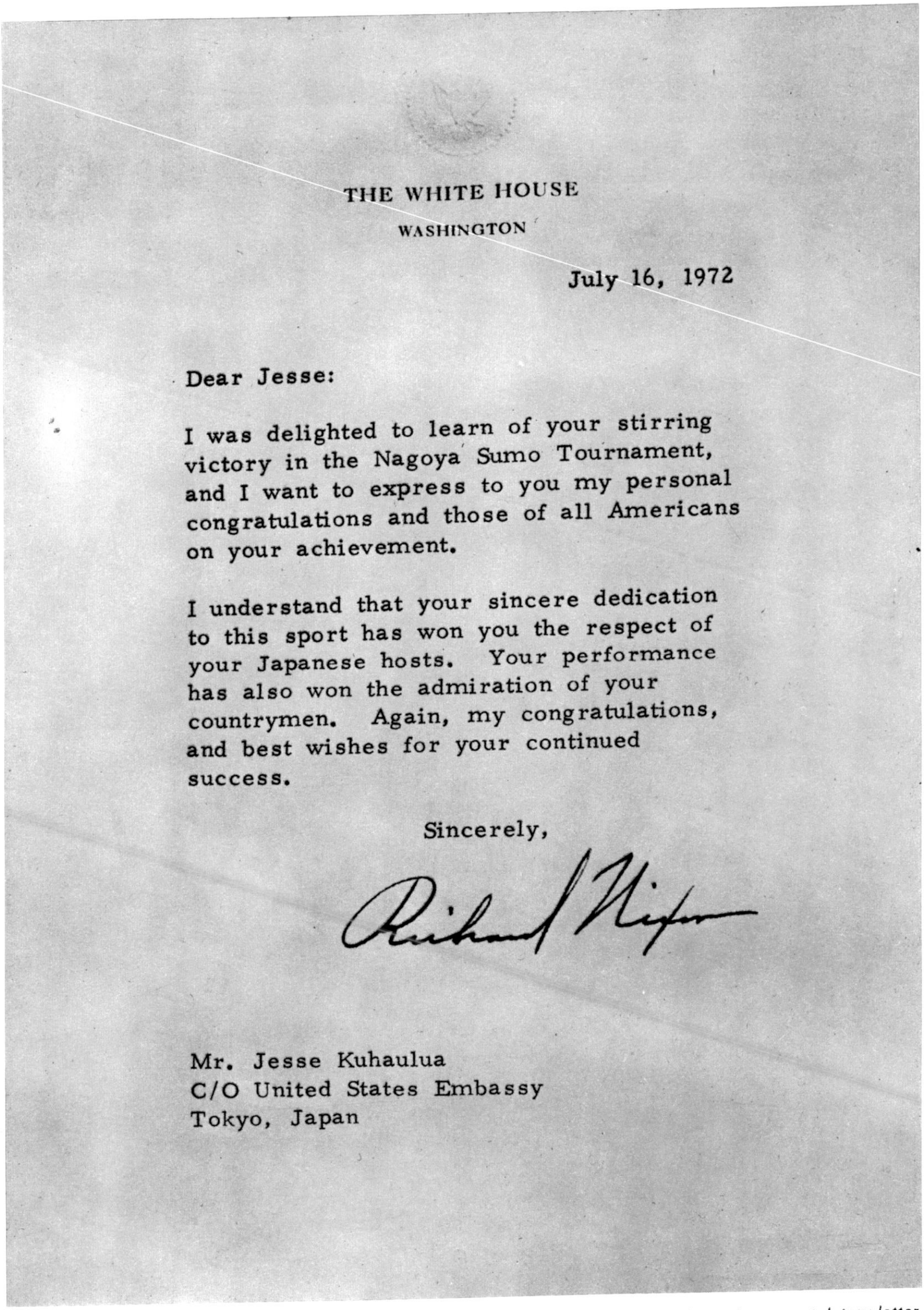

THE WHITE HOUSE

WASHINGTON

July 16, 1972

Dear Jesse:

I was delighted to learn of your stirring victory in the Nagoya Sumo Tournament, and I want to express to you my personal congratulations and those of all Americans on your achievement.

I understand that your sincere dedication to this sport has won you the respect of your Japanese hosts. Your performance has also won the admiration of your countrymen. Again, my congratulations, and best wishes for your continued success.

Sincerely,

Richard Nixon

Mr. Jesse Kuhaulua
C/O United States Embassy
Tokyo, Japan

President Nixon's congratulatory letter.

above the thunderous applause. Standing beside the ring as the first strains of the Japanese national anthem fill the hall, I think of how many times I have watched other wrestlers receiving the championship trophy that in a moment will be mine, of how many times I have dreamed of standing in their place myself. Is the dream continuing or is this time for real? It's hard to be sure.

Still dazed I climb up on to the ring. But this time, instead of a grim-faced opponent, I face the President of the Sumo Association standing behind the enormous Emperor's Cup, symbol of the championship. We bow. He hands me first a certificate and then the huge cup itself. Too excited to hand the certificate on before taking the cup, I find myself crumpling it slightly against the trophy. An assistant reminds me as I pass both down to him, and I promise to observe proper formality with the trophies to come. I guess I can be forgiven one slight slip up, I hardly had time to practice.

The prizes and cups follow in rapid succession, the championship flag from which a banner hangs down bearing my name along with the names of winners of recent tournaments; the Prime Minister's Cup; a crystal bowl, symbol of friendly relations between Japan and Czechoslovakia, presented by the Czecho-slovakian ambassador; a huge framed portrait that will hang in the sumo arena in Tokyo together with those of other recent champions; a cup from Japan's largest broadcasting network. Then, near the end of the presentations, my close friend David Jones, director of public relations in the Far East for Pan American World Airways, comes up to award the Pan Am trophy. Dressed in formal ki-mono, he reads the certificate in Japanese and presents the award as he does at the end of every tournament. But this time he departs from the script to add a few remarks in English about the special joy and satisfaction he feels today since in his many years of making the award he had always hoped that one time I would be the recipient. Shaking his hand, I am conscious again of tears that begin to well around my eyes.

Just as I prepare to leave I am told there is one more event on the program. The tall, lanky American ambassador to Japan, Robert Ingersoll, has made a spe-cial trip to Nagoya to personally read a message of congratulations from the United States. Fighting tears and disbelief, I stand with him in the center of the ring as he reads the letter.

"Dear Jesse: I was delighted to learn of your stirring victory in the Nagoya Sumo Tournament, and I want to express to you my personal congratulations and those of all Americans on your achievement. I understand that your sincere dedi-cation to this sport has won you the respect of your Japanese hosts. Your per-formance has also won the admiration of your countrymen. Again, my congratu-lations, and best wishes for your continued success. Richard Nixon."

As I hurry back to the dressing room to change for the parade through the city and the victory celebration, I can still hear the ambassador's words and become momentarily convinced that this whole thing must really be a dream after all.

I

Kokugi

Today

During those fifteen long July days in Nagoya, I was thrown into the dirt or pushed out of the ring only twice: In my other thirteen bouts, it was I who did the victorious pushing and throwing to become the first non-Japanese, the first *gaijin*, ever to win the Emperor's Cup in Japan's *kokugi*, national sport. My battleground was an unroped, eighteen-foot-square, two-foot-high mound of clay called the *dohyo*, its hard surface covered with a thin layer of sand. Sumo bouts are confined to an inner circle about fifteen feet in diameter delineated by round, straw, earth-filled bales sunk into the clay protruding only a few inches above the ground. In training, *sumotori*, as sumo wrestlers are called, work out in practice rings which, apart from the protruding bales, are flush with the ground. Injuries can occur, though they very rarely do, when two huge men topple simultaneously over the edge of the two-foot-raised tournament dohyo.

Sumotori fight unarmed and almost naked, their only covering being the mawashi, a heavy piece of silk approximately ten yards long by two feet wide which is folded in four and then wrapped around the waist and groin. Hanging down from the mawashi in front is the purely ornamental *sagari*, a short string skirt composed of starch-stiffened lengths of silk. Practice mawashi, with which the sagari is not worn, are made of cotton and are white if the wrestler is in one of the top two divisions of the sport, and darker if he is not. But the mawashi is no mere concession to modesty or colorful decoration. It is rather the key to most of the sport's throwing and forcing techniques which involve maneuvering the opponent after securing a grip on his mawashi. There are wrestlers who have done very well by consistently employing tactics, such as pushing or thrusting, which do not involve grabbing the mawashi. I, myself, don't use it as much as I should. Sumo's greatest stars, however, are usually highly skilled on the belt.

The object of the sport which I decided to make a career is deceptively simple. A sumotori wins when any part of his opponent's body, other than the soles of his feet, touches the dirt inside the ring or when any part, even a single toenail, touches outside the straw circle. Since the goal in sumo is either to throw, push, trip, or pull the opponent down inside the ring or to carry, push, or force him outside it, there is none of the horizontal grappling leading to points or a pin as in many other forms of wrestling. After going through a series of limbering-up exercises and ceremonial acts, the two wrestlers face each other in the center of the ring, assuming an aggressive crouch. On the referee's signal they charge, crashing together with a fearsome smack. This initial charge, the *tachiai*, when two huge men rush at each other with total force, is the moment of truth in sumo. The tachiai generates a feeling of intense excitement and exhilaration and is for the lover of sumo what the long touchdown pass is to the football fan.

Fights are usually brief, most are over in less than a minute. The shortest—such as when one sumotori sidesteps the other's charge and pulls him down on all fours—last little over a second. Contests lasting several minutes usually involve fierce maneuvering for a favorable hold on the mawashi, which is then used to throw the adversary or force him outside the circle. One of sumo's most thrilling sights is watching a wrestler secure a belthold with both his hands under the opponent's arms (*morozashi*) and then proceed to lift the hapless fellow off his feet and deposit him outside the straw (*tsuri-dashi*). Equally dramatic is *utchari*, a backward pivot throw which snatches victory from defeat and symbolizes very well the speedy, chancy, unpredictable nature of the sport. Utchari is employed by the sumotori who has been driven back to the edge of the ring and seems certain to be pushed out. At the last second, the apparent loser braces his feet against the straw rim, leans precariously backwards, and, twisting his body, lifts the attacker off his feet and swings him around his own body and out of the ring. His opponent is forced to touch outside seconds before he himself topples over backwards into the first row of spectators. Tsuri-dashi and utchari are only two of the seventy official winning techniques listed in 1960 by the Sumo Association, professional sumo's controlling body, but they provide excellent illustrations of the power, speed, and dramatic reversal of fortune that pack the brief moments of struggle in the dirt ring.

Undoubtedly the most striking thing to the first-time spectator of a sumo bout is the size and shape of the sumotori. Although the day of the four-hundred-pounders seems over, most wrestlers tip the scales today at somewhere between 230 and 380 pounds. Right now, I'm the tallest man in the sport at 6' 4" (190 cm) and also one of the heaviest, usually weighing around 360 pounds (163 kg). Most of the massive bulk of the sumotori is concentrated in the lower part of the body. A unique combination of highly rich food and specially designed exercises produces a physique characterized by thick legs, heavy hips, and a large, protruding belly. The basic aim of this remarkable theory of body-building is to create a low center of gravity for balance and stability, to put a man in the ring who is difficult to push around and even harder to topple. As the ultimate key to success in sumo is said to lie in the wrestler's *ashi* (legs) and *koshi* (hips), coaches spend the greatest number of hours putting their sumotori through workouts designed to strengthen these two areas, and sportswriters are quick to evaluate the strength or weakness of a wrestler's *ashikoshi* in analyzing his prospects. Another basic goal in raising a champion is producing a body that, while capable of great strength, is also flexible and supple. A tight, stiff, muscle-bound sumotori, no matter how strong, would be an easy victim for his opponent's throws and unable to flow smoothly with the quickly changing course of the bout. The ideal body is one that covers a very considerable muscle development with a thin layer of fat. Largely because of their huge bellies, many sumotori seem just plain fat when viewed from a distance. But, although there are a few almost pathetically corpulent men in the sport, anyone who has gotten close enough to try socking a sumotori in the stomach will gladly go back to brick walls.

Not all wrestlers are behemoths, however. Some are "small," weighing a mere 220 or 230 with little stomach protrusion. And these lightweights find themselves up against the 350-pounders. For while professional sumo is divided into six divisions which are further subdivided into ranks, the classifications have nothing to do with weight. Skill alone leads to advancement up sumo's pyramid-like rank structure, and there are both big and small sumotori at all levels. The absence of weight divisions provides an added element of excitement for the sumo enthusiast, who often has the thrill of watching a wrestler outmaneuver and defeat an opponent almost twice his size.

There are virtually no regulations controlling entry into the sport. The only exception is the minimum size requirement governing recruits. An aspiring sumotori of eighteen or younger must be at least 170 centimeters (5′ 8″) tall and weigh at least 70 kilograms (154 lb.); for those recruits over eighteen the lowest limits are 173 centimeters (5′ 9″) and 75 kilograms (165 lb.). If size limitations are minimal, so too are the number of things a sumotori is not allowed to do in the ring. Sumo is really more remarkable for the actions that it does allow than for those it does not. Nearly everything goes in the sport including tripping, slapping with the open hand, and even pushing hard under the opponent's chin with an extended arm (as long as the fingers are locked open and there is no attempt to grab the throat). Among the few fouls which lead to automatic defeat are punching, purposely pulling by the topknot hairdo which wrestlers wear, thrusting fingers into the eye, clapping both ears simultaneously, choking, grabbing that part of the mawashi covering the private parts in front or the thin strip between the buttocks in back, and applying bone-breaking pressure such as bending the fingers back with full force.

Today, sumo is probably one of the most bloodless contact sports in the world. The referee is even allowed to give the combatants a breather to prevent total exhaustion. If a bout has continued for some time with neither sumotori able to break through the secure hold of his opponent, the referee may step in and call a *mizu-iri*. He stops the action, separates the wrestlers, allows them a few moments rest, and then replaces them in exactly the same position with the same holds. But such has not always been the case in sumo's long history. The predecessor of the modern sport was a much more rough-and-tumble affair with some bouts, literally, fought to the finish.

Yesterday

Sumo is as old as Japan and the gods who created her. For more than fifteen hundred years sumo has, in one form or another, played an important part in the fabric of Japanese life. The sport's name, rules, dress, techniques, and fortunes have inevitably varied with the ebb and flow of historical events as well as with the changing values and patterns of social organization, but it has always endured as a vital expression of the Japanese spirit.

Like so many other aspects of Japanese culture, the origins of sumo are shrouded in the rich folklore of the nation's myths and legends. From Japan's oldest literary monument, the *Kojiki* [Records of ancient matters], completed in A.D. 712, we read that in the early struggles among the gods for dominion over the land, the fate of the "divine race," which eventually triumphed and produced an imperial line that is claimed to be unbroken to this day, once hinged on the outcome of a test of strength. It seems that the sun goddess, Amaterasu, dispatched Take-mika-duti-no-kami (Brave-Awful-Possessing Male Deity) to wrest control of the "Central Land of the Reed Plains" (Japan) from the diety Opo-kuni-nushi-no-kami. The defense of Opo-kuni-nushi-no-kami's realm was entrusted to his second son, Take-mi-na-kata-no-kami (Brave-August-Name-Firm Deity). Donald Philippi has translated the outcome of that fateful contest:

"...Take-mi-na-kata-no-kami came bearing a tremendous boulder on his finger-tips and said:

'Who is it who has come to our land and is talking so furtively? Come, let us test our strength; I will first take your arm.'

When he allowed him to take his arm, he changed it into a column of ice, then again changed it into a sword blade. At this he was afraid and drew back.

Then (Take-mika-duti-no-kami), in his turn, demanded (the right) to take hold of the arm of Take-mi-na-kata-no-kami.

When he took it, it was like taking hold of a young reed; he grasped it and crushed it, throwing it aside. Immediately he ran away.

They pursued him, and caught up with him by the lake of Supa, in the land of Sinano; as they were about to kill him, Take-mi-na-kata-no-kami said:

'Pray do not kill me. I will go to no other place...I will yield this Central Land of the Reed Plains in accordance with the commands of the offspring of the heavenly deities.' "

While little of what we call sumo today can be seen in such cosmic hand-shaking, the fact that a trial of strength between two combatants was given such a crucial role in the Japanese myth cycle by early writers reflects the significance such contests must have had in the beliefs and customs of the early Japanese, long before the scholars of the *Kojiki* took their brushes in hand. Philippi sees the test of strength as a kind of litigation in which disputes were settled by divine will. Indeed, *sumapi* (an early name for sumo) was in ancient Japan a ritual performed to discover the will of heaven, as were similar contests in primitive societies elsewhere. Other writers see an added dimension in the *Kojiki* story, that of the magnanimous spirit of the wrestler in pardoning the vanquished. This spiritual side is still as intrinsic a part of sumo today as the physical aspects.

From fragmentary archeological evidence (such as baked-clay statuettes, or *haniwa*, in the form of wrestlers excavated from burial mounds), local folklore, and another early historical document, the *Nihongi*, we can surmise that an early kind of sumo ritual was performed by the rice cultivators of the Yayoi and Kofun periods (200 B.C.–A.D. 552) to divine the outcome of the harvest. Supporters of the winner could expect divine grace and good crops; those on the losing side were in for trouble. These contests, called *shinji-zumo*, show that from the earliest times sumo was closely associated with religious rites—and with the shrine, the center of such activities—together with the agricultural practices which molded the Japanese character. And when such struggles were staged before the imperial court, their meaning began to assume national importance.

The *Nihongi* [Chronicles of Japan], completed in A.D. 720, covers early history from the period of the gods through the reign of Empress Jito which ended in 697. The first of several references to wrestling describes a deadly bout in 23 B.C., in the seventh year, seventh month, seventh day of the reign of Emperor Suinin. W. G. Aston's translation tells us that certain courtiers informed the emperor of a man named Kuyehaya from the village of Taima "of great bodily strength," who could "break horns and straighten out hooks" and who would boast: " 'You may search the four quarters, but where is there one to compare with me in strength?' " The emperor asked if there was anyone who could challenge this "champion of the Empire." A brave man named Nomi-no-Sukune was suggested, and the emperor immediately ordered a contest. The two warriors were brought together and "stood opposite to one another. Each raised his foot and kicked at the other, when Nomi-no-Sukune broke with a kick the ribs of Kuyehaya and also kicked and broke his loins and thus killed him."

The fatal contest between Kuyehaya and Sukune has often been described as the beginning of sumo's development, because it is the first recorded match in Japanese history between mortals. Sukune is enshrined by many as the founder of Japanese wrestling, though it's lucky for today's sumotori that the rules have been tightened a bit since his day. And the legend, greatly embellished through countless retellings long before the authors of the *Nihongi* wrote it down, lives on, cherished in the folklore, and the hearts, of many Japanese. Legends often play an equal role with history in a nation's literature, and this is especially true in Japan. Even today a large sumo festival is staged, every year on the seventh of July, at the place where the classic struggle is said to have taken place.

The *Nihongi* tells us of another legendary bout which took place in A.D. 469 although the wrestlers were incidental to the story. Apparently, a carpenter called Mane of the Wina Be used to plane timber with an axe, using a stone for a ruler. "All day long he planed and never spoiled the edge by mistake." The Emperor Yuryaku, hearing of his fame came to see him. He asked, " 'Dost thou

A woodblock artist's impression of a sumo bout between Kawatzu Saburo and Matano Goro which took place in 1176 in front of the Shogun Minamoto-no-Yoritomo. The print dates from the late Edo period.

never make a mistake and strike the stone?' Mane answered and said, 'I never make a mistake!' Then the emperor called together the Uneme, and made them strip off their clothing and wrestle in open view with only their waistcloths on." Mane was intrigued and looked up from his planing for a moment or two. When he resumed he unwittingly made a mistake, and the emperor triumphantly rebuked him: "Where does this fellow come from that without respect to us, he gives such heedless answers with unchastened heart?"

Whether the point of the story is that watching wrestlers quickens the blood, or whether it's just meant to show that you don't get smart ideas in front of the emperor, I don't know, but, happily, the poor man lived to see more wrestling, for a plaintive poem from a fellow carpenter moved the emperor to reconsider his order for Mane's execution.

In later sections of the *Nihongi,* closer to the time in which the compilers of the chronicles actually lived, we find more verifiable accounts of wrestling matches. In A.D. 642, Empress Kogyoku commanded "stout fellows" to wrestle before envoys from Korea. Forty years later, during the reign of Emperor Temmu, the *Nihongi* relates that "Hayato (palace guards) came in numbers with tribute of the productions of their country. On this day the Hayato of Ohosumi and the Hayato of Ata wrestled in the Court. The Ohosumi Hayato had the victory." And in A.D. 695, Empress Jito "witnessed wrestling by the Hayato at West Tsuki no moto."

During the reign of Emperor Shomu (724–749), famed builder of Nara's Great Buddha Hall, wrestling matches at the imperial court became part of formal ceremonies held every year on the seventh day of the seventh month. *Sumai* (sumo), together with court dancing, concerts, and other entertainment were held in an open plaza in the presence of the emperor and high-ranking nobles. With the groundwork laid by Shomu, wrestling quickly became an independent court ceremony during the Heian period (794–1185). Called *sumo-sechie*—together with archery and mounted archery one of the three sports "sechie" officially established during the period—these elaborate, annual wrestling pageants continued for over three hundred years, securing sumo's reputation as a national sport.

But the sumo-sechie was not merely a spectacle to amuse the court or a device to encourage the military development of the nation. It was also an important religious rite, a national form of the shinji-zumo which had been practiced since ancient times to divine whether the Heavenly Will would provide luck and good crops.

The wrestlers who performed at the sumo-sechie were largely farmers, conscripted throughout the nation by imperial command. They belonged to one of the two barracks of imperial guards, left or right. Before the day of the sumo-sechie, seventeen combatants were chosen to represent each camp. Unlike today, each man fought as a member of a team, and the victory went to the side, left or right, which won a majority of the seventeen bouts. According to their camp, wrestlers entered the fighting area from the left or right side of the emperor (today's east and west). Rankings were few, but the top man from each camp was given the title *hote* and the next best two that of *waki*. The other wrestlers were known as *sumaibito*.

As in early local forms of shinji-zumo, there was no referee at the sumo-sechie. Instead, two men from each of the two camps were selected to bring the wrestlers together and start each bout. Another dramatic difference from today's sumo was the absence of a dohyo. The dohyo, which confined the action to a limited space, was a much later development which profoundly changed the sport by creating the possibility of victory through forcing the opponent out of the ring. But during the age of the sumo-sechie and for some time thereafter, the sole aim of sumo was to topple the enemy off his feet. Such toppling was, however, made less violent through the introduction of rules prohibiting such techniques as kicking and punching. In fact, it was during this period that most of the basic throwing techniques we see in the sumo ring today were born. These refinements, carried out under the continuing patronage of the imperial court, divorced sumo from its "no-holds-barred" origins and brought it much closer to its modern form.

The many miraculous stories and anecdotes concerning sumo in the Heian period make for delightful reading. One of the most interesting, recorded in the *Gempei seisuiki*, tells of a succession dispute between two sons of Emperor Montoku (850–858), Koretaka and Korehito. It was decided to settle the quarrel through a sumo bout which looked on the surface to be a terrible mismatch. Chosen to represent Koretaka was a giant named Ki-no-Natora who possessed the strength of sixty men; named as Korehito's delegate was a tiny man named Ootomo-no-Yoshio. When the two wrestlers came together the huge Natora grabbed Yoshio and threw him into the air, but Yoshio managed to straighten his body before he landed and came down still on his feet. Hearing of Yoshio's danger, the chief priest of a nearby temple began to pray. Suddenly, a huge water buffalo, bearer of dignity and virtue, appeared and began to let out a great bellow which carried all the way to the palace and caused all the strength to leave Natora's body. Seizing this unexpected opportunity, Yoshio quickly threw Natora to the ground and secured the throne for Korehito.

As the influence of the imperial court waned and political power shifted to the military classes during the twelfth century, sumo ceased to be a court function. But the sport continued to prosper under Japan's new masters. Called *buke-zumo* (warrior sumo), wrestling was promoted by the samurai as a necessary military art for fighting men, along with archery and swordsmanship. Prominent wrestlers often served under military commanders on the battlefield leaving behind records of great daring. Since primary emphasis was placed on its value as martial training and its effectiveness as a battlefield technique, buke-zumo assumed a quite different form from the earlier wrestling ceremonies at the court. Victory was granted to the man who not only toppled his opponent but also rendered him helpless by pinning him to the ground. In this sense it probably

more closely resembled some types of wrestling prevalent in the west than modern sumo. Judo, which had remained undifferentiated from sumo for hundreds of years, gradually began to come into its own as a separate military art by the sixteenth century, finally becoming a fully independent form by the outset of the Tokugawa period (1603–1867).

Parallel with sumo's inclusion as one of the martial arts for military training—and far more important in the development of the modern sport—was the popularization of wrestling matches as entertainment which began during the Kamakura period (1185–1333) and continued to the time of Oda Nobunaga (1534–1582). The founder of the military government in Kamakura, Shogun Minamoto Yoritomo, was said to have seen sumo matches together with mounted archery and horseracing as part of a festival at the Kamakura Tsurugaoka Hachiman Shrine in 1189, setting a precedent for other military leaders. And in local areas throughout the country, wrestlers returning home informed the populace of the sport's refined techniques and spread its popularity. Sumo bouts took place in temple and shrine compounds all over the land continuing the shinji-zumo tradition. But by this time wrestling matches were primarily entertainment. The shrine would benefit from the spectators' donations. And in return, temple officials would share the proceeds with the wrestlers who drew the crowds. These performances, called *kanjin-zumo* (sumo to solicit funds for pious purposes) from about the middle of the Muromachi period (1336–1573), gave rise to semi-professional groups of wrestlers who toured the countryside plying their trade at religious festivals before both warriors and commoners. During the same period, less formal bouts, known as *kusa-zumo*, were held in village fields, deepening sumo's roots among the people.

It was during the Tokugawa period that sumo became fully professionalized in the expanding urban centers and took on the form we know today. Apart from a few notable exceptions, with the advent of professional groups of wrestlers, first in Kyoto and Osaka and later in the military capital Edo (Tokyo) wrestling matches as part of religious festivals were discontinued. The name kanjin-zumo was retained, but the matches were staged to put money into the pockets of the wrestlers and their supervisors, not to raise donations for religious bodies. In the early years, sumo bouts in cities like Edo were often the scenes of bitter quarreling and fighting among the samurai in attendance, prompting the Tokugawa government, during the years 1648 to 1720 to issue, occasionally, decrees prohibiting the performances. Despite the bans, sumo's popularity remained undiminished, and promoters often staged matches on street corners (*tsuji-zumo*) and in temple compounds without permission. But such precarious employment was hardly enough to fill the wrestlers' rice bowls. To save their livelihood, professional sumo groups, in an effort to remove the causes of the disputes surrounding their performances, worked out a series of rules and regulations to govern the sport and selected supervisors to enforce them. Winning techniques were carefully defined and the matches were confined to a limited area, the dohyo, as they are today.

These efforts finally led to official sanction—as early as 1684 in Edo itself—for kanjin-zumo.

At the outset of the Tokugawa period, the best wrestlers were employed by Japan's great feudal lords, given samurai status, and treated like retainers. When the prohibitions on wrestling went into effect, the lords temporarily lost interest in sumo, but it was soon rekindled with the revival of kanjin-zumo during the Genroku era (1688–1704). Leaders of various fiefs encouraged professional wrestlers by giving stipends to physically well-endowed subjects and tried to bring successful kanjin-zumo combatants to their fiefs to enhance the glory of their domain. Rich merchants also contributed to the sport's prosperity by giving money to their favorite wrestlers. Through such continued patronage, sumo as a professional sport came into its own.

Although there were independent sumo organizations in several parts of the country, the most important center of kanjin-zumo exhibitions during the Genroku era was the Kyoto-Osaka area, and it was there that a system of official tournaments and rankings was worked out. By the 1780s, however, when sumo had become fully organized on a national basis, the capital had shifted to Edo. Wrestlers came from all over Japan to participate in the great Edo tournaments launching sumo into an unprecedented golden age and laying the groundwork for the modern sport.

By confining wrestlers to a prescribed area, the dohyo, sumo became almost a different sport. For with the emergence of the circular ring, a new series of techniques, aimed at forcing the opponent beyond the straw boundary, joined the classical toppling skills to make the sport faster and more complicated and much more exciting for the spectator. There are many theories about the origins of the dohyo. At the end of the Muromachi period bouts took place within a circle formed by seated spectators and victory went to the wrestler who either threw his opponent within the circle or pushed him into the crowd. But since a human boundary hardly makes for precise delineation, and probably caused some painful moments for those unfortunates in the first few rows, it was decided to mark the battlefield with straw bales (hyo). Some sources place the construction of the first dohyo in the early 1570's, during the supremacy of Oda Nobunaga, said to have been a great enthusiast of the sport. Nobunaga's official annuals, however, make no mention of the dohyo, and the first time the dohyo makes an appearance in sumo drawings and pictures is during the decade after 1673. The earliest rings were made by simply placing the bales on the ground to form either a square or a circle. Later, during the early eighteenth century, the bales were partially buried and the circular shape was fixed, establishing the form that has continued to the present day.

When the Black Ships of Commodore Matthew Perry landed in Japan in 1853, signaling the beginning of the end for the Tokugawa government and its closed-door policies, huge sumo wrestlers were mobilized to show the unwelcome intruders the size and strength of the Japanese nation. The following year, upon the return

Right, *The legendary Raiden, against the only Ozeki ever to beat him twice (c 1795). Below, The classic bout between Sukune and Kuyeheya (23 B.C.). Left, The first Takamiyama, later the first Takasago, sumo reformer and founder of Takasago-beya.*

of the American ships, wrestlers went to the port of Yokohama to try to further intimidate the persistent strangers by lifting and carrying heavy rice bales, staging bouts, and throwing with ease those sailors foolish enough to accept the challenge. It is recorded that one huge sumotori by the name of Shiramayumi managed to load eight bales at once on to a ship by somehow balancing four bales on his back, two in front of his chest and one in each hand. While such feats of strength must have duly amazed the foreign sailors, the wrestlers' efforts did little to change Perry's determination that Japan open its doors to the West.

The years immediately after the Meiji Restoration of 1867 were difficult ones for sumo. With the abolition of the old fiefs and establishment of national prefectures, samurai patrons of the sport, who had supplemented the tournament income of the good wrestlers by employing them as bodyguards and in other capacities, were thrown on hard times. The rapid reforms of the new government also created a sense of uneasiness among many people who had previously contributed to sumo's prosperity, causing attendance at the tournaments to fall off. Moreover, the early Meiji years saw a sudden craze for "civilization and enlightenment," for all things Western, and a rejection of many elements of the nation's past that were seen as obstacles to rapid development. Caught up in these revolutionary waves, sumo was denounced as an anachronistic holdover from Japan's feudal days. Newspapers took up the cry, arguing that the "uncivilized" sport should be abolished and that the near nakedness of the wrestler was ugly and shameful. In the face of such challenges, officials of the old Edo sumo organization, the *Sumo Kaisho*, while vowing not to let the sport die, could offer little in the way of constructive counterproposals.

With the continuation of the sport in doubt, a champion of reform finally came forward in the person of a high-ranked wrestler named Takasago. Anxious to do away with some of the evils that plagued the Sumo Kaisho and to breathe new life into its organization, Takasago pressed for changes—only to find himself expelled from its councils. Undaunted, he went to Nagoya and set up his own organization, returning to Tokyo in 1876 to stage a demonstration exhibition in Akihabara. Failing at first because the Tokyo police would not allow two sumo groups in the city, Takasago gradually won the sympathy of some influential people, who strove to reconcile his differences with the older sumo body. These efforts finally paid off in Takasago's reinstatement in the organization and a series of reforms in its management. Takasago soon became the head of the Sumo Kaisho, and after completely revamping the old Tokugawa period organization, changed its name to the *Tokyo Ozumo Kyokai* (Tokyo Sumo Association) in 1889. Wrestlers performed for the organization and in turn shared the proceeds with its administrators. This body was the forerunner of the modern *Nihon Sumo Kyokai* (Japan Sumo Association) which controls the sport today.

It was the same Takasago who founded what was to become one of sumo's most prosperous stables (places where wrestlers live and train), which still bears his name. Over eighty-five years later, the same Takasago stable became my home after I left Hawaii and came to Japan to seek my fortune in the sumo ring. The sumo name I was given, Daigoro Takamiyama, reflected the high hopes my coaches had for me: it was the original wrestling name of the stable's founder, before the pioneer reformer changed it to Takasago.

While men like Takasago labored from the inside to keep sumo alive, winds of change began to blow in society at large. The headlong rush to Westernization produced an inevitable counterreaction by those seeking to prevent Japan's traditional culture and characteristics from being swept away entirely. A key turning point for the national sport came in 1884 when Emperor Meiji, a practitioner of sumo himself, had an exhibition held in his presence to emphasize his support. And in the years after 1885, sumo benefitted from a new sense of national confidence and patriotism that was solidified by Japan's victories in war against China and Russia. The sport's complete recovery was symbolized by the successful completion in June 1909 of a permanent home for sumo tournaments, the Kokugikan (Hall of the National Sport) in the Ryogoku section of Tokyo. Before the Kokugikan was built tournaments had been held in a makeshift structure which had a small roof supported by four pillars over the ring but left the spectators at the mercy of the elements. The present home of sumo, also called Kokugikan, is a postwar structure located in Kuramae, just across the river from the home of the original Ryogoku building. It is the site of the three tournaments held in Tokyo every year in January, May, and September. Three additional tournaments are held annually outside Tokyo in Osaka (March), Nagoya (July), and Fukuoka (November).

From about 1910, there had been plans to remove one of the last remaining irrationalities in sumo's organizational setup. There were two independent sumo associations, one in Tokyo, the other in Osaka, with each holding independent tournaments and occasional joint ones. Basic differences in the constitution of the two groups prevented a merger until 1925. In April of that year, with a gift of money from the crown prince, the Tokyo Sumo Association created a victory cup (the Emperor's Cup) to be presented to the winner of each tournament. The argument that the honor of presenting the imperial award should not belong to Tokyo alone finally broke the negotiation deadlock. The creation of the Japan Sumo Association at last brought the administration of the sport under a unified national body.

The first recipient of the Emperor's Cup was grand champion Tsunenohana, winner of the January tournament in 1926. Forty-six years and 178 tournaments later, I had the honor of being the first non-Japanese to receive that same cup. The newspapers the day after the tournament proclaimed that a new but still unfinished page was being written in the long history of Japan's kokugi, but it was hard for me to think on such a grand scale. I knew, only, that the championship was the proudest moment in my sumo career which had begun some thirteen years earlier in the amateur sumo rings of my native island of Maui.

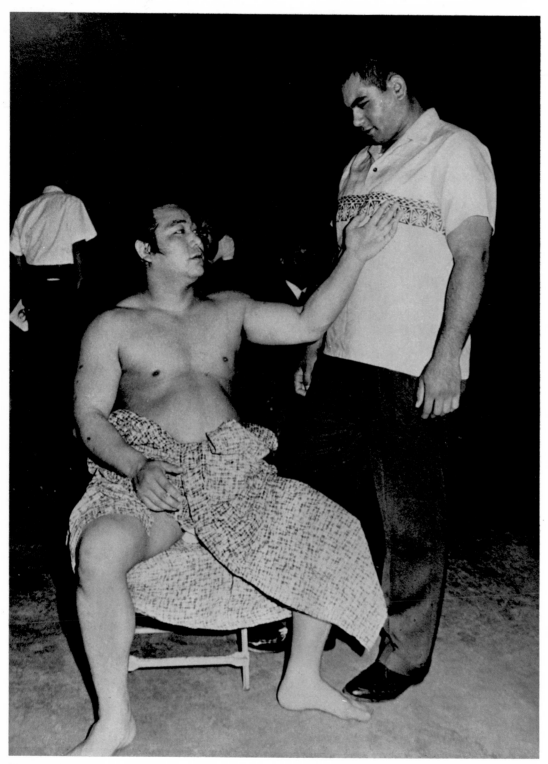

Hawaii, February 1964. Yokozuna Tochinoumi helped persuade Takamiyama to come to Japan and become a sumo wrestler.

II

Happy Valley
to Takasago-beya

Maui: The first nineteen years

Why? I don't know why, maybe it was fate, but looking back it seems amazing that I ever became a professional sumo wrestler. The reasons that I took up the sport in the first place were a second-grade accident and a desire to play high school football, and had nothing to do with any positive interest in sumo itself. At least in the beginning. But I'm getting ahead of myself.

I was born Jesse James Walani Kuhaulua on June 16, 1944, in Happy Valley on the island of Maui. I've heard that I weighed ten pounds, fourteen ounces, and I must have kept up the pace because I remember always being much bigger than the other kids. I was the oldest of what was to become a family of five children, three girls and two boys. My family is of Hawaiian ancestry, and I remember not being able to understand very much of their conversation when I visited my mother's relatives because they only spoke Hawaiian. Many people today think that I must have Japanese blood, too, because of my ability to adapt to Japan and the sumo life, and some stories I have read have claimed that I am of Japanese descent. It's not true, but I suppose in one way it's a compliment.

Money was tight from the beginning. But with everybody pitching in to help, we got by. There wasn't enough, however, to buy luxuries, like a television set, and I remember when I wanted to watch T.V. I'd go to the drugstore. I used to stand outside the store and watch through the window for hours at a time. I knew then that I'd have to work awfully hard if I was going to get where I wanted. One of the things I recall most clearly from those early years was how hard I worked. Whether it was chores around the house or cleaning yards and cutting grass for neighbors, I used to really buckle down. I was certainly more serious about working than I ever was about school. Although I goofed off in the classroom once in a while, I would never do that when I was working. Part of the reason was of course the need for extra money, but my size and strength led me quite naturally to physical things. I was a good worker and so I enjoyed it. In the seventh grade at Iao School, when I started working as a gardener, I was 6′ 1″ and weighed about 260 pounds. From my freshman year in high school, I worked part-time for a man who repaired washing machines. My job was to carry the machines from private homes to the truck.

Not having an allowance made if difficult to come by much spending money. One method I used to save a bit was to forego lunch at high school. Since my mother gave me twenty-five cents for lunch money every day, I could pocket a quarter by not eating at noon. I didn't seem to lose any weight by it. And sometimes if I needed spending money for a trip with the football team, I could ask my grandfather. There was always food on the table, but I had to do without many other things. I remember being embarrassed always having to ask the neighbors to borrow a basketball or football when I wanted to play or going to classes my freshman year in high school with large holes in the bottom of my shoes because I couldn't afford new ones.

There were, of course, good times as well during my school years. During junior high at Iao School and later at Baldwin High, I used to hang around with four other guys. Two of them eventually had cars, so we spent a lot of time just driving around, taking turns at the wheel. Sometimes, when my family wasn't home, I'd invite them over and do some cooking. We all chipped in to buy the food. Nothing fancy, just rice and canned stuff like pork and beans, sausages, or corned beef, but I liked to cook and at the time we all thought it tasted great. I had many other friends too. I guess I was one of the most popular guys at school. My uncle has said that although I was bigger than the other kids, I was good-natured and could fit in to any group. I don't know. I've always liked many different kinds of people. And, besides, there weren't too many people willing to pick a fight with me anyway. But I do remember being very shy with the girls. If I did any dancing at the high school dances it was because the girls would come to ask me. I didn't really go out with a girl until my senior year at Baldwin. Maybe I should have been a bit more aggressive because I wasn't bad looking. Big, but I sure didn't have the stomach I do now.

From a quite early age, the thing I wanted to do the most was sports. Being big and strong, I should have been a natural for things like football and track and field, but I always had a problem with weak legs. During second grade at Wailuku Elementary School I was in a hurry going to school one day and ran across a road without looking. A truck hit me and threw me about twenty yards, badly injuring both my legs. I was in the hospital for about six months and couldn't go to school. I gradually began to walk again, but only after being in a wheelchair for three or four months. Even after I went back to school, I could never keep up with the other kids because my legs would quickly tire and begin to hurt when I ran. I tried out for the softball and track and field teams later at Iao School, but I couldn't make it.

I thought at one point that I'd never be able to be involved in team athletics. And it wasn't until my freshman year in high school that I finally made a team. Coach Larry Shishido of the Baldwin High Bears was quite understandably impressed with my size—I was about 6' 2" and close to 280 pounds in my freshman year—and gave me a chance to play football. Although it was still difficult to run long distances, I did pretty well as a tackle, and became an all-star co-captain in my senior year. At one point during that senior year I got up a little over three hundred pounds, and the coach would sometimes use me in the backfield when we were goal-to-goal within the ten or when we needed the extra yardage. I usually made it because everyone was afraid to tackle me. I guess I was the only three-hundred-pound fullback in Hawaii. Later I put the shot and threw the discus for the track team.

Coach Shishido was also the one who got me to try sumo. To strengthen my legs, he suggested at the end of my freshman year that I take up weightlifting and sumo. Since he himself was involved with sumo, he knew that the sport's basic exercises, which concentrate on the hips and legs, would help me where I was weakest. So I joined the Maui Sumo Club under the head instructor, Isamu Ogasawara. The club is one of several amateur sumo organizations in Hawaii supported by first- and second-generation Japanese intent on keeping alive the customs and traditions of their heritage. Like similar clubs in Honolulu and on the big island of Hawaii, the Maui group practices sumo for about one month every year in preparation for an inter-island tournament. The best seven wrestlers from each club are sent to the tournament which is held alternately on one of the three participating islands either on June 11, the birthday of King Kamehameha, unifier of the Hawaiian islands, or on the fourth of July. On years when the tournament is not held on Maui, the Maui Sumo Association and other groups of Japanese descent sponsor Japanese films and cultural events to raise money to send the Maui team to Oahu or Hawaii.

During my first year of sumo practice, I was picked as one of the seven men to represent Maui in the inter-island tournament. Each wrestler in the tournament fights as a member of his team. There is no individual champion crowned and there is no ranking of the wrestlers as in Japanese professional sumo. Maui didn't win that year but I won my matches. Although I didn't have a lot of finesse, I could usually overpower my opponent with a hard charge and a pushing and thrusting attack. I found sumo interesting, but I was still in it largely to help my football—and, if possible, to win prizes. Every year at the tournament there were prizes awarded for performance in the bouts which preceded the main bouts to decide the championship team, prizes like canned goods, radios, and trophies. A wrestler putting together a string of three straight victories was eligible for a prize, a wrestler winning five in a row would win a better prize, and so on.

With the help and instruction of Ogasawara and two brothers named Aloha and James Sato, I gradually learned more and more about sumo and began to really enjoy the sport for its own sake. During the month before the next tournament the following year we practiced twice a week from six to ten in the evening and I never missed a session. But the real turning point came later that summer, in August of 1961, when three instructors came from Japan to work with Hawaiian wrestlers. The head of the Japanese group was Professor Toshio Takizawa, athletic director of Tokyo's Meiji University. He was accompanied by two former college sumo champions, one of whom was the Japanese amateur champ. Since they planned to take a group of Hawaiian wrestlers back to Japan with them to fight against Japanese university and amateur wrestlers, the main purpose of the visit was to teach the Hawaiians the finer points of the sport, such as what to do in the ring before the bout starts and the proper way to toe the mark just before the initial charge.

While preparing the wrestlers for their trip to Japan, the Japanese instructors spent a week in each of the Hawaiian sumo centers, Honolulu, Hilo, and Maui. During their stay on Maui, I turned out for training every day and I think I impressed Takizawa. Although there were other guys at the workouts who were also big and maybe as good as me, the combination of my size, youth, and attitude—Takizawa said I was *majime* (serious, dedicated)—particularly excited him. I was quite flattered when he asked me to come to Japan, but I had to refuse because I was still in school and didn't have the money.

It was Takizawa who finally made me go bare. He and the other Japanese instructors were appalled to find that some of us younger guys tied the mawashi over a pair of shorts. Many of the older wrestlers didn't seem to mind wearing only the mawashi, which leaves most of the hip area exposed except for a thin strip between the buttocks, but the younger guys were shy and a bit more hesitant. So we wore the shorts, too. But the Japanese, to whom our appearance must have looked quite ridiculous, would have none of this concession to American modesty. Takizawa told me that he wanted to take some pictures of me to show to people back in Japan, but that I'd have to remove my shorts. I was quite embarrassed but I did what he said and felt for the first time what it would be like to be a real sumotori.

The instruction and praise I received from the Japanese instructors provided the key incentive to work harder at sumo. And although I didn't really believe at the time that I would ever have the chance, Takizawa's invitation to go to Japan filled my head with dreams of foreign travel and visions of triumphs in the sumo ring that went far beyond beating Oahu or Hawaii in the inter-island tournament. Little did I know how soon those dreams would come true.

When Takizawa returned to Japan he showed the pictures he had taken of me to his friend Takasago, the former grand champion Maedayama and boss of Takasago-beya. I heard that Takasago expressed interest and said that he would like to have the opportunity to see me in person. But there the matter rested for over two years. During that time I completed my last two football seasons for Baldwin and just before graduation, in May 1963, joined the National Guard under a six-year obligation. Training with the guard for six months after graduation, I began to lose weight for the first time, coming down from the 300 plus pounds of my fullback days to a mere 240 or so by the beginning of 1964. A real lightweight, at least by my standards. I also spent about a month loading fruit crates onto trucks and trains for the Maui Pineapple Company. And, of course, I continued to think about sumo and practiced when I had the chance.

In February 1964, Takasago led a group of Japan's top pro sumotori to Hawaii to give exhibition matches in Honolulu. Because the Japanese athletes also planned to give training to local wrestlers, Ogasawara arranged with the Maui Sumo Association to take me over. He said that there were four candidates from Oahu who were trying to break into sumo in Japan and that since Takasago had already expressed interest in me I should have the chance to go and get a taste of tough competition. Tough competition is putting it mildly. It was more like a Little Leaguer trying to hit a home run off Sandy Koufax or strike out Willy Mays. But my first chance to get in the ring with sumo's best, including Taiho, one of the greatest grand champions in the sport's history, was a thrill I will never forget, even though I have since fought against Taiho and the others for real in Japan. As we Hawaiian wrestlers struggled in vain against the pros, Takasago and Furiwake(the former grand champion Asashio and then a coach of Takasago-beya)watched us carefully. The trained eyes of the two men were not looking for wins and losses, however; they noted youth, size and technique, and searched for that elusive but all-important quality of determination. I must have scored well because after showering at the end of the first day's session I was taken to meet Takasago and Furiwake. And Takasago wasted no time in formally inviting me to come to Japan and join his stable.

My first reaction was shock and disbelief. Although I soon found myself saying yes, I'll go, I wasn't really thinking about sumo. Maybe it was because I was so young and had always dreamed of going abroad like any kid, but my head began to swim with all the good things I'd read and heard about Japan in Hawaii, about the country, the people, the girls. I wanted to go and see Japan for myself and here was my chance. My excitement did abate enough, however, to allow me to tell Takasago that I couldn't make a final decision until I talked with my family. The next day, after training once again with the Japanese sumotori, I returned to Maui for the funeral of my grandfather. At home I met with strong opposition from my mother. I was, after all, the eldest son and I could understand her feeling that I should stay home and work rather than seek some wild, uncertain future as a wrestler in faraway Tokyo. But I was now determined to go and tried patiently to explain that sumo was my chance to be something, a success, and that I would not disappoint her. Members of the Maui Sumo Association also helped, spending a long time explaining that I could do very well in the sport and in the process promote good will between Hawaii and Japan. Reluctantly, Mother gave her consent.

I spent the next two weeks getting ready to leave. Takasago and the Japanese wrestlers left Hawaii for exhibitions in San Francisco and Los Angeles, and I was supposed to meet them a week later at Honolulu airport on their way back to Japan. But my visa didn't come in time to go with them. Another temporary stumbling block was my six-year commitment to the National Guard of which I had completed less than a year. But the 442nd Veteran's Club, descendent of the famous Nisei regiment that had distinguished itself in action in Italy during World War II, supported my decision to enter sumo and interceded with the governor of Hawaii for my release. It was obtained on the provision that I would be subject to the regular draft after my first year in Japan. The way was finally cleared for my departure. The night before I left, the Maui Sumo Association and other friends gave me a farewell party. There was a lot of talk about the hardships and discipline of life in a sumo stable and of the odds against me as a foreigner. But although I had often heard how rough it was, I was too keyed-up that last night on Maui to feel worried or nervous. I was about to embark on a great adventure in Japan, and if there was hardship involved, what the hell. I wasn't even thinking that much about the sport I had decided to make a profession. My heart was just too full of excitement and anticipation. For I knew I would really be on my way tomorrow. The next day, February 22, 1964, I flew west from Hawaii, leaving behind the life I'd known there for nineteen years.

Tokyo: The first four days

The following day I learnt what winter is. For the first time in my life I stepped into a cold, harsh wind as it blew across Tokyo's Haneda Airport. Shivering, I greeted Takasago. Conscious only of the cold and the unreality, I was taken downtown to my new home, Takasago-beya, a rambling, unheated wooden structure where some sixty wrestlers lived and trained. The huge tatami-mat rooms where the wrestlers spread out their *futon* (bedding) to sleep, heated only with small gas or kerosene stoves, seemed all the more cold and foreboding in their emptiness: most of the men in the stable were away on tour. On my second day in Tokyo, I was amazed to see snow falling outside the window. It was the first time I had ever really seen it. In Maui it snows every few years or so on one mountain top, and everybody runs out to see it. But now I know it isn't much to get excited about.

The cold is really all I can remember about those first few days. The small stoves were only just sufficient to take the chill off the rooms during the day, but since the danger of fire in those wooden buildings is too great to leave a stove burning unattended, it must be turned off at night. In the morning it was like waking up inside a refrigerator. Clambering up off the futon into that freezing air was a daily agony. It was hard, too, at least in the very beginning, to get used to a life without furniture. There were no chairs and the low tables could only be used while sitting cross-legged on cushions placed on the tatami. It was not living on the floor itself that was difficult for me—tatami mats have a lot of give to them. The painful thing was sitting for any length of time with my legs tucked under me. I'm sure any large man who first samples the Japanese life-style will readily understand. And I'm a whole lot bigger than most large men.

There was no training, however, since there were only ten wrestlers who were not on the tour. Everybody treated me really well, trying to make my introduction to a totally new environment as easy as possible. The first three nights Mrs. Takasago cooked American food, things like ham and eggs and chicken, and I slept in the room reserved for the heya's top-ranking wrestlers. I didn't realize until later what very special treatment this was for a new recruit. Looking back now, those first few days, despite the newness of everything, were perhaps the most comfortable moments of my first three years in sumo.

Four days after I arrived in Japan, I left Tokyo to join the rest of the stable in Osaka to begin training there for the Osaka tournament, held every March. It was there that I began to find out what the life of a professional sumotori was all about.

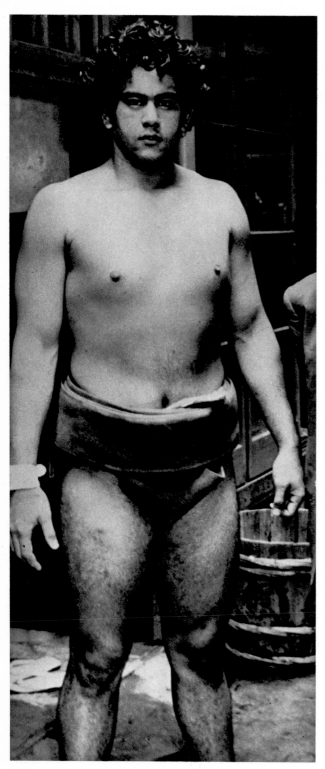
Jesse soon after he arrived in Japan.

III

Sumodo

Shingitai

When older Japanese gather over steaming cups of saké to talk about their national sport, they often use the word *sumodo* instead of the more common and shorter form, "sumo." The Chinese character used to write the *do* of sumodo means way or path, both in the concrete sense of street or thoroughfare and the more abstract sense of a life course or pattern of moral conduct. Examples abound in the language, among them *bushido* (the way of the warrior), *shinto* (the way of the gods, Japan's native religious form), *kendo* (the way of the sword, swordsmanship), *shodo* (calligraphy), *sado* (the way of tea as embodied in the tea ceremony), and *judo* (the flexible way). Similarly sumodo (the way of the wrestler) gives expression to a particular value system which underlies the more physical and technical aspects of the art of sumo. For sumo is more than a sport. It is in reality a way of life which places as much emphasis on sound and vigorous spiritual and emotional development as it does on physical training.

The three key elements in the success of a sumotori are said to be *shin* (mind, heart, spirit), *gi* (art, technique), and *tai* (the body, physique). Often used together to form the word *shingitai,* these three essentials may be said to lie at the core of sumodo. And the meaning implicit in the fact that *shin* stands as the first part of shingitai is not lost on the wrestler who aspires to the heights of sumo. Wakanohana, one of the most successful and popular grand champions of the postwar period and currently boss of his own stable, remembered his first realization that size was not everything. When he was a child, Wakanohana followed avidly the exploits of a grand champion whom all sumo experts concede to be the greatest of all time, Futabayama, holder of the almost unbelievable record of sixty-nine straight victories. But since there was no television in those days, Wakanohana never saw Futabayama in person until he joined the sumo world and after the great champion had retired from the ring. Before meeting Futabayama, Wakanohana had met another wrestler named Dewagatake who stood over 6' 6″ and weighed close to 450 pounds. Since Dewagatake never became a grand champion, Wakanohana imagined that such a brilliant grand champion as Futabayama must certainly be an even more imposing figure than the man-mountain he had met. When he was finally introduced to Futabayama, Wakanohana could hardly believe it. "He looked only a little bit bigger than an average

man. I just couldn't believe that this was the man who had won sixty-nine
straight. But it really was Futabayama. I realized then that sumo was not body.
It was spirit."

While one very important element which characterizes sumodo is fighting spirit
in the ring, another is the high value placed on manners and courtesy. Wakanohana, who has written on the philosophy of sumo, has said that the sumo manner
is the spirit which begins and ends with etiquette. Arrogance has no place in a
world which stresses respect toward one's superiors, the proper forms of address,
modesty and humility, and the ability to take what is dished out without display-
ing weakness or unnecessary emotion. It would be hard to imagine a sumotori,
no matter how strong and confident, bragging before a bout about how he was
going to demolish his opponent the way Muhammad Ali might. The wrestler who
has just slammed his victim into the dirt will extend an arm to help the enemy
to his feet and both men will bow to each other before leaving the ring. The
elation of victory or agony of defeat are rarely evident on the faces of combatants
as they descend the ring and leave the arena. Such emotions are released in more
private surroundings, away from the public glare. This forbearance may be one
reason why some people think sumotori, who are normally great talkers in informal situations, do not express themselves very well—especially in television
interviews just after they have won an important bout. The wrestler usually
makes some modest comment about being lucky or just having had a good day
and then responds with a nod of the head or a grunt as the interviewer tries to
answer his own questions. For a wrestler to analyze the weak points of his victim,
particularly if he has just upset a high-ranked champion or grand champion,
or to praise his own effort would be both disrespectful and in bad taste.

Sumo etiquette extends to all aspects of the wrestler's life both inside and outside the ring. From such seemingly minor considerations, but important to
the opponent, as keeping the body clean and the fingernails cut short, to the
proper way to formally receive messengers from the Sumo Association on that
great day when a triumphant wrestler is officially informed that he has been
promoted to the lofty rank of grand champion, the sumo code of conduct is carefully defined. The code places a high premium on correct relationships between
superiors and inferiors. The young apprentice who has been given training by
a high-ranking wrestler in his heya will offer him a ladle of water as a gesture of
thanks. The upper wrestlers, in turn, will offer water to the stable boss and
coaches at the end of practice. Should one coach politely refuse the drink, the
wrestler will not then offer the same ladle to the next one; he will empty the
undrunk but nonetheless "used" portion and go back to the water bucket to
refill the ladle afresh. After the highest wrestlers in the heya have had a bath,
finished the noon meal, and retired to their rooms to rest, they will be visited
briefly by the youngest apprentices who, one by one, bow at the entrance and
give a formal greeting that might be translated as "You must be very tired."

The hierarchical, rank-conscious world of sumo is of course reflective of the national culture which gave it birth. As social anthropologist Chie Nakane has pointed out, Japanese society is characterized by a vertical principle governing human relationships. But while Japan's rapid democratization, and urbanization since the Meiji period have caused great changes in the society's tight vertical structure, the world of the wrestler, by nature a closed and highly protected society outside the modern cultural mainstream, has been less affected.

This is not to say that significant changes have not taken place. One of the most profound was the introduction in 1957 of a guaranteed monthly wage according to rank, although only sumotori in the sport's two top divisions are eligible to receive it. Moreover, present-day wrestlers wear Western clothes more often than their prewar counterparts and many now prefer whisky to saké and meat to fish. Some have enough money to own color television sets and stereos and enjoy such leisure pastimes as golf and bowling, much like their contemporaries in other walks of life. But to reach a rank high enough to enjoy such amenities as a salary—and many never make it—a young recruit entering a stable at fifteen or sixteen must endure long years of harsh training and strict discipline in the paternalistic environment of the stable. In return for his board and lodging and in the belief that it will infuse him with the proper moral rectitude and fighting spirit necessary for success, the apprentice is expected to help keep the stable clean, prepare and serve the meals, and be at the constant beck and call of the coaches and high-ranking wrestlers for everything from back-scrubbing in the bath to running errands. Through service one learns the ropes at first hand and becomes worthy of being served later on. The onerous duties provide the incentive to work hard in the training ring to reach as soon as possible a rank which entitles one, in turn, to such service.

Thus, despite slow but inevitable change, sumo society is still much closer to its feudal past than most other areas of modern Japan. One distinguished and long-term enthusiast of the sport has commented that since the breakup of the old Japanese army, there are only two places in Japanese society where the old-fashioned, strict class system still survives: in some of the nation's underworld gangs and in sumo. While this may overstate the case, it is true that the feudalistic demands placed on the aspiring sumotori, together with the financial uncertainty of becoming a professional sumo wrestler, have made it increasingly difficult to find recruits for the sport. In 1963, the year before I entered Takasago-beya, 250 youngsters decided to make sumo a career. Eight years later, in 1971, the number of boys joining sumo stables had fallen to 156, forcing many heya to run recruitment ads in newspapers. And of those who do give sumo a try, many find the going too tough and drop out. The total number of professional sumotori had dropped from a peak of over eight hundred in 1959 to just over five hundred and fifty by the end of 1972.

Although sumo is not in danger of dying, indeed, it is currently enjoying renewed popularity owing to the exploits of a few glamorous, young stars, there are many who argue that the sport will face a crisis if it does not become more democratic, both socially and financially. They complain that often unreasonable demands are made on young apprentices by their superiors and that the sport's profits are not divided fairly between the officials of the Sumo Association on the one hand and the wrestlers, *gyoji* (referees), *yobidashi* (attendants who call out the wrestlers' names before each bout and perform other services), and stable hairdressers and assistants on the other. Others insist that while necessary reforms have been and will be made, extreme care must be taken to preserve sumo's unique character. They fear that changing the nature of sumo society too radically and making life too comfortable for the recruit would destroy that elusive but all-important spirit which lies at the core of the way of the wrestler and which alone can forge true champions. It would take the "do" out of sumodo. Some older purists moan that this has already happened, that a stoic and noble discipline capable of producing heroic men has fallen victim to a mass media-oriented, comfort-loving modern culture. But nostalgia for a golden past does little to confront the problem of changing times and tastes. One of the most remarkable things about the long history of Japan's national sport has been its ability to withstand sometimes fundamental change, to survive and remain vital. And it will continue to flourish for many years to come.

Despite its feudal elements, there exists in sumo a kind of basic democracy not found even today in more modern areas of Japanese society. This is the value placed on ability, regardless of age or experience. Wrestlers in the top two of professional sumo's six divisions, *juryo* and *maku-uchi,* no matter how young, are known as *sekitori* and earn the right to forego chores, earn a regular salary, and have stablemates in the bottom four divisions serve them personally as *tsukebito* (literally a "person attached," but meaning a kind of servant at the beck and call of another—all non-sekitori wrestlers are assigned to a certain sekitori or heya coach as tsukebito). It is purely on the basis of ability that the speed of a wrestler's rise up the rank pyramid is determined. A sumotori named Kitanoumi set a record recently by becoming a sekitori at seventeen. The great Taiho set another by reaching sumo's highest rank of *yokozuna* or grand champion at twenty-one. Though a seventeen-year-old sekitori would still remain polite and respectful toward a twenty-eight-year-old wrestler in a lower division and not make unnecessary demands on him in deference to his greater experience, it is the older man who helps the younger into his kimono when the sekitori goes out or ties the sekitori's mawashi in the dressing room before tournament bouts.

The banzuke

Since a sumotori's rank determines everything from his status to his salary, let us take a look at the sumo ranking system. The major divisions, in descending order, are shown on the top of page 51.

The lowest grouping, *maezumo,* is not really a division and does not appear on the *banzuke,* a list of official ratings published by the Sumo Association prior to each tournament. Maezumo combatants are young recruits who have just joined

Sekitori		MAKU-UCHI DIVISION	The First Class (within the curtain)
	Sanyaku	Yokozuna	Grand Champion
		Ozeki	Champion
		Sekiwake	Junior Champion
		Komusubi	Junior Champion, 2nd grade
		Maegashira	Senior Wrestlers
		JURYO DIVISION	Contenders (ten-*ryo* men)
		MAKU-SHITA DIVISION	The Second Class (below the curtain)
		SANDANME DIVISION	The Third Step
		JO-NIDAN DIVISION	The Second Step
		JO-NO-KUCHI DIVISION	The First Step
		MAEZUMO	Pre-sumo

sumo stables. They wrestle during the first half of each fifteen-day tournament (*basho*) under a point system in an effort to climb to the first rung of the sumo ladder, *jo-no-kuchi*. Two consecutive wins on one day entitles the victor to one point; a total of four points ensures promotion to jo-no-kuchi for the following tournament. Only a wrestler who wins his first bout of the day is entitled to a second, but should he subsequently lose, he earns no points and must try again the following day. Those who fail to accumulate four points during a tournament must wrestle again in maezumo at the next basho.

Each of the six divisions above maezumo is divided into a series of numbered ranks with two wrestlers—one who fights from the east side of the ring, the other from the west—holding each rank. Taking juryo, the second highest division, as an example, there are usually twenty-six sumotori contending, although the number may be slightly less in certain tournaments. These twenty-six men hold thirteen ranks. Because the east is deemed a bit more prestigious than the west, the top man in the division is east number one, the next west number one, the next east number two, and so on down to the lowest man at west number thirteen. The four divisions below juryo follow the same pattern although the total number of wrestlers in each (and thus the number of ranks at east and west) is quite a bit larger than in juryo. Juryo and *maku-shita* used to be a single division, and even today they occupy the same line on the banzuke, although the names of juryo wrestlers are written in slightly larger characters. The name "juryo" means ten *ryo*. During the Tokugawa kanjin-zumo period, wrestlers were paid a daily salary of about one ryo (about fifty U.S. cents at that time) when they first appeared in a tournament. Through consistent victories and promotions, a sumotori could gradually increase his earnings. Men who received ten ryo a day were known as juryo. Today, the jump from maku-shita to juryo is a crucial one because it means passing from the status of struggling wrestler to that of sekitori, with all the benefits that status entails.

The highest division, maku-uchi, commands the most attention of the average supporter, for it is here that the very best wrestlers are assembled and it is the bouts in this division alone which are carried daily on national television. The maximum number of men in the division is set at thirty-eight, but at most tournaments the number is slightly less. The bulk of the division is comprised of sumotori called *maegashira* who, like juryo wrestlers, are divided into ranks from one to about thirteen from both east and west. Above the maegashira, in the rarified atmosphere near the top of the sumo pyramid, are the three *sanyaku* ranks of *komusubi, sekiwake,* and *ozeki.* Towering above everyone at the summit are the yokozuna. Unlike the system of having two wrestlers for each rank which holds true from maegashira on down, there can be and often are more than two wrestlers at each of the top four ranks. Sometimes there are less.

Promotion and demotion depend on a wrestler's performance at each basho. Except for the two top ranks of ozeki and yokozuna, a majority of wins, *kachi-koshi,* at a tournament almost invariably means promotion for the next one; a majority of losses, *make-koshi,* usually results in demotion. For the sumotori in the four divisions below juryo who fight only seven times during a fifteen-day basho, the magic number of wins is four. For the sekitori in juryo and maku-uchi who fight every day, it is eight. The more victories above four or eight that a wrestler can achieve, the more rungs that can be advanced in a single leap. Similarly, those with the most defeats will fall farthest. The sumotori lives under the constant threat of demotion. For under the harsh reality of the ranking system, he must prove himself anew at each tournament, six times a year.

This was brought home to me in a particularly personal way long after I had become a sekitori myself. Asaarashi, a fellow sekitori and one of my best friends at Takasago-beya, fell briefly from juryo to maku-shita, losing his sekitori status, and was assigned as tsukebito to me. He was not only a personal friend, but also had been a sekitori a year longer than I had. I didn't like the idea of Asaarashi serving me. But since it is custom that the senior tsukebito wrap the sekitori's mawashi in the dressing room before tournament bouts, it was Asaarashi who had to help me. It was a funny feeling. Fortunately he went back up to juryo soon afterwards.

The two exceptions to the kachi-koshi, make-koshi rule involve promotion to ozeki and yokozuna. The word ozeki means "great barrier," and for those wrestlers who make it to the sekiwake rung just below, it is exactly that. Since it is on the shoulders of the men who become ozeki and yokozuna that the prestige and honor of the entire sport rests, the Sumo Association will elevate to sumo's top ranks only those wrestlers who it thinks can not only consistently win an overwhelming majority of their bouts but also conduct themselves in a manner worthy of the rank. A wrestler qualifying for promotion to ozeki has usually held his sekiwake rank for several tournaments with a record of ten wins or better. As an ozeki, he must then continue to perform outstandingly and should win the Emperor's Cup two or more times to be considered for yokozuna. An ozeki can be demoted only if he fails to make kachi-koshi in two consecutive tournaments, but he will usually retire rather than suffer such disgrace. A yoko-

The wooden banzuke *and tower outside Kokugikan. From the top of the tower a* yobidashi *beats a drum to open and close each tournament day.*

zuna can never be demoted, but he, too, will retire when he is no longer able to uphold the honor of his rank. Because of the stiff qualifications for promotion, the number of ozeki and yokozuna varies greatly from year to year. For example, at the outset of 1953 there were five grand champions, at the end of 1972 only one. There have even been brief periods when no one held sumo's highest rank. By January 1973, history had recorded only fifty-three yokozuna from the time the title was created in the Tokugawa period.

Yokozuna take their name from a thick white length of rope (*tsuna*) which they alone are allowed to wear during ceremonial appearances. The rope's weight varies with the girth of the wearer, but it is probably well over twenty pounds. It takes as many as six or seven assistants, each wearing white gloves to avoid sullying the sacred length, to pull the tsuna tight around the yokozuna's middle and then tie the elaborate bow in back. This exercise has reminded some people of the dressing of a prize bull. Hanging down from the rope in front are zigzag strips of white paper called *gohei*. Although usually much smaller, similar ropes decorated with gohei are found in Shinto shrines, over gateways, and in small shrines in private homes, and are symbolic of the guardian deities of production, the *musubi-no-kami*.

The origins of the yokozuna rank are difficult to pinpoint. One fanciful legend holds that the first historical yokozuna, Akashi—who is thought to have lived in the early Tokugawa period but about whom very little is known—felt embarrassed about his nakedness on being presented to the emperor and grabbed a rope hanging in a temple precinct to cover himself. More reliable accounts begin with the Anei era (1772–1780) when one or two of the strongest ozeki (at that time the highest rank) were often called to participate in ground-breaking ceremonies for castles and estates. Ropes were stretched on the ground to divide the good land from the bad and over them the wrestler would stomp the earth with his feet (an exercise, seen in the sumo ring to this day, and meant to drive away evil spirits). To purify their own bodies, wrestler participants in such ceremonies wrapped ropes called *musubi-no-kami-no-o* around their waists. Later, during the Kansei era (1789–1801), certain ozeki were given official permission to perform individually a kind of stylized dance prior to matches held in the presence of the Tokugawa shogun and members of his house. (This ceremony, now called the *yokozuna dohyo-iri*, is still performed today.) Because they wore the tsuna during their performances, the ozeki so honored received the title of yokozuna. This title was completely ceremonial, however, and had nothing to do with rank. Ozeki was still the highest rank in sumo, and even those who obtained permission to perform as yokozuna before the shogun were listed on the banzuke as ozeki. While it is true that those designated ceremonial yokozuna were often the strongest ozeki of their day, this was not always the case. One of the greatest and most legendary ozeki, Raiden, never became a yokozuna. Although many are fond of repeating the famous story that Raiden was too rough to wear the tsuna because he had killed an opponent by breaking his ribs, the fact is that he, like others, just never had the chance to perform before the court. And since Raiden already held the sport's highest rank and the awe of his age as the strongest wrestler, there was no need to go out of his way to seek a title that was purely ceremonial. The first time the title yokozuna appeared as a separate entity on a banzuke was in 1890 during the Meiji period. By 1903, the rank of yokozuna had been recognized as the highest in sumo.

One confusing element in the sumo ranking system is the distinction between east and west. We have seen how in the days of the sumo-sechie wrestlers belonged to barracks of either the left or right (east or west) and fought as members of a team. Although minor changes were made, team-style competition continued over the centuries, until it finally gave way to the individual free-for-alls of modern times. Today, wrestlers are still divided into east and west on the banzuke published before each basho. From yokozuna on down, the assigning of direction to men of equal rank is based on their performances at the previous tournament. The man on the east at any given rank is slightly higher than his counterpart on the west, but the distinction is almost nominal. When there are more than two wrestlers at a given rank, as often happens at the top four rungs of the sumo ladder, the names of the two men with the best records at the last basho appear on the banzuke in the normal east and west positions while those of the "extras" are projected out to the sides (*haridashi*), creating such rank names as "east haridashi ozeki," "west haridashi sekiwake," and so on.

Officials making match pairings no longer take into consideration the east-west distinction, and thus a man from the east is just as likely to be fighting a fellow east-sider as he is an opponent from the west. When possible, a sumotori will enter the arena and ascend the ring from the direction to which he is assigned. But should he be fighting an opponent of higher rank from the same direction, he must yield to his superior and fight from the opposite side. The two wrestlers' dressing rooms (*shitaku-beya*) are also designated east and west, but each wrestler uses the dressing room of the direction from which he is fighting that day, not necessarily the one at which he is listed on the banzuke for the entire tournament. Even in the colorful entering-the-ring ceremony, performed by both the juryo and maku-uchi divisions before the commencement of their respective bouts, the east-west distinction is confused. Although the ceremony is carried out in two parts, with half the division performing from the east and half from the west, the wrestlers enter the arena from their dressing rooms. So a man could be with the east group one day and the west the next.

One final and extremely severe element of the ranking system, modified only very recently, is counting as losses those days when a sumotori is unable to appear because of sickness or injury. Since a majority of losses means demotion, a wrestler with a serious injury who misses many consecutive tournaments could fall from the top division all the way to the bottom of the ladder, and many men drag themselves into the ring when they should be resting. Moreover, with six basho a year there is little recovery time between tournaments. There have been periodic clamors for reform, but the issue came to a head in October 1971, when a powerful yokozuna with a bright future, Tamanoumi, died suddenly after undergoing a routine appendectomy. Although appendicitis and complications from the operation were the immediate cause of death, it was disclosed afterwards that Tamanoumi had been suffering other ailments as well as his appendix problem for some time, but had nonetheless continued to appear in tournaments and carry out his many other social responsibilities as a yokozuna. It was pride and the desire not to disappoint that kept Tamanoumi going, since as the holder of sumo's highest rank he was not threatened with demotion. Other lower-ranking wrestlers have ascended the dohyo with sprains, fractures, or serious illness.

Tamanoumi's death and the outcry it provoked provided the final incentive to create the occupational accident system (*kosho seido*), established in January 1972. This system allows the wrestler who has sustained an injury during a tournament to remain out of the succeeding basho without loss of rank. The decision on whether to recognize the injury as kosho or not is made by Association officials after a medical examination has been carried out. But the system is still only partial, because it is limited to only the tournament following the one in which the wrestler was injured. If the injured man is still not able to wrestle in succeeding basho, his nonappearance days again count as losses, as under the old system.

Heya and oyakata

Any account of sumodo must discuss the sumo *heya* or stable and the men who run it. For it is in the heya that sumotori live and train and it is here that the values and manners of the way of the wrestler are inculcated. Only married men are permitted to live outside, but they, too, spend much of their time at the heya practicing, eating, or simply relaxing.

The practice of retired sumotori (*toshiyori*) raising young wrestlers dates from the early Tokugawa period, when professional sumo became an independent occupation. The beginning came in 1684 when an early organizer of professional sumo, Ikazuchi Gondaiyu, received official permission from the Tokugawa government to stage kanjin-zumo exhibitions. With the birth of wrestling as a full-time occupation came the need for administrators, and this job fell to certain toshiyori. Over the next century, the work of the toshiyori was gradually systematized. When the first banzuke was printed in Edo in 1757—banzuke appeared even earlier in Kyoto—the names of three toshiyori supervisors appeared along with the names of the wrestlers and referees. During the next fifty years, the number of toshiyori, as well as the duties they were expected to perform, greatly increased. These responsibilities included administering and promoting the sport, staging tournaments and exhibitions, and, perhaps most important of all, recruiting and training young wrestlers. The toshiyori also organized a body to control sumo.

Today, every aspect of sumo is controlled by the toshiyori members (or *oya-kata* as they are more commonly called) of the Japan Sumo Association, an incorporated foundation under the Ministry of Education. Since becoming a toshiyori provides employment and the chance to remain in the only world they have known from the age of fifteen or sixteen, most wrestlers are anxious to join the association when they retire from the ring, usually around the age of thirty. But the door is not open to everyone. To qualify for oyakata status, a retiring sumotori must have wrestled one or more tournaments in the top maku-uchi division or, if he had never risen higher than the juryo level, have wrestled in that division for either twenty consecutive basho or a total of twenty-five basho or more. What's more, a new oyakata must purchase "stock" in the Association (the *toshiyori kabu*) at a price said to be about fifteen million yen (over $45,000).

This stock, the capital for which usually comes from the wrestler's patrons and support groups, gives the buyer the right to assume one of the 105 established toshiyori names upon his retirement. But since the number of names, and thus the number of toshiyori, is limited to 105 at any one time, the aspirant must wait for the death or retirement (at sixty-five) of one of the existing oyakata if the quota is full. The money for the stock is paid to the retiring oyakata—or to his heirs if he has died—by the new oyakata who receives his name.

The only time that there can be more than 105 oyakata is when the association decides to make a rare exception to honor an extraordinary individual such as a yokozuna who has left an exceptionally brilliant record. This happened in May 1971 when the great Taiho retired. He was allowed to become the 106th oyakata, and to keep his wrestling name as a toshiyori. The exception expires with the death of the man honored, and is known as *ichidai yokozuna* (one generation yokozuna). When Taiho dies not only will his name not remain in the association for another oyakata to buy, but it can never again be used by another active sumotori as can most wrestling names.

The large number of men who do not qualify when they decide to hang up the mawashi must find employment outside the world of sumo. Since most wrestlers become excellent cooks during years of preparing meals in their stables, many go into the restaurant business. But for those who cannot make it on the outside, the story is often a sad one. Sumotori who have not made the grade have little chance to save, since there is no regular salary for men in divisions below juryo. They also cannot attract their own patrons and fan clubs—a primary source of income for successful sekitori—and the retirement benefits that do exist, again, are only for sekitori. The association may grant a special retirement bonus for meritorious service, but yet again it is usually only the more successful wrestlers who are honored.

In the past the only thing the unsuccessful sumotori is said to have received when leaving the heya was a railroad ticket back to his home and a thank-you. While this is no longer true if in fact it ever was—all sumotori receive a kind of severence pay if they have appeared in fifteen or more tournaments, although the amount is pitifully small for those below the juryo level—the communalism which characterizes the world of the heya usually ends abruptly with retirement, except for those who enter the association. Wrestlers are guaranteed all the basics of their livelihood by the stable boss for as long as they can hold their own, even if they remain in a low division for most of their career. But after that, they are on their own. Like rank, money and security accrue to the wrestler on the basis of results, and results alone.

The Sumo Association controls every aspect of the sport. Headed by a president and board of directors selected from their ranks, its members arrange tournaments and both national and overseas tours, serve as judges at every basho, supervise the referees, operate Kokugikan which houses the association's offices and is the scene of the three Tokyo tournaments every year, fix and pay the salaries and other stipends of wrestlers and oyakata, and serve as stablemasters and coaches. Like the sport it represents, the association has been accused of being feudalistic with its emphasis on seniority, its resistance to change, and in its almost absolute control over the wrestlers and their finances. While this may be true, the critics often belittle the many, if still only partial, reforms that have been made. The fixed salary system has made at least sekitori wrestlers far less dependent on the whims of their oyakata than in the past, and the harshest aspects of heya life have gradually disappeared.

Further democratization will undoubtedly creep in. But the members of the association are, after all, former wrestlers who have been through it all themselves and naturally feel they know best how to keep the modern sport both alive and profitable without throwing away completely a way of life and system of values that not only is capable of producing great champions but also is seen as a positive force in molding character. Abolishing the heya, throwing open the management to private enterprise or government bureaucrats, and making the wrestlers independent agents with full collective bargaining rights, would undoubtedly bring Japanese wrestling into the twentieth century. But it would no longer be sumo.

The wrestlers themselves have not always been silent when they thought their treatment was unjust. There have been strikes by sumotori three times in the twentieth century in 1911, 1923, and 1932, largely over demands for better financial distribution and retirement benefits. Demands were drawn up and sent to the association and some wrestlers actually tried to set up independent organizations to stage matches.

Most dramatic was the 1932 protest, called the Shunjuen Incident. Under the leadership of sekiwake Tenryu, the entire west side of the maku-uchi division together with eleven juryo wrestlers drew up a series of resolutions just before the January basho. When their demands were rejected by the association, the Tenryu group cut off their topknots, resigned from the association, and formed an independent sumo organization. Soon afterwards nine maku-uchi and eight juryo sumotori from the east side also resigned from the association and formed

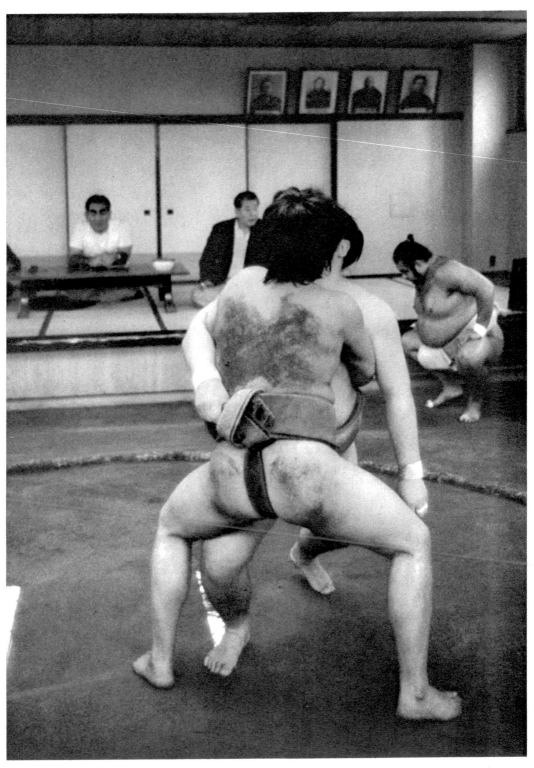

Oyakata Takasago (the fifth) presides over morning training at Takasago-beya. In the top right are photographs of the four Takasagos who have preceded him.

still another reform sumo body which cooperated with the Tenryu group. With well over half the maku-uchi division and much of the juryo division gone, the association resorted to the drastic measure of elevating to the highest division a number of juryo and maku-shita wrestlers in order to stage the tournament, which was finally held in February to an almost empty house. In desperation, the association offered some concessions, and by the following year most of the rebels were back in the fold, and the crisis over. Tenryu and a few diehards, however, refused to return, and took their protest to Osaka. There they formed an organization called the Kansai Sumo Association which lasted for a short time until 1937.

Today, wrestlers in the top two divisions belong to a kind of quasi-union called the Rikishi Kai, headed by a yokozuna. Though the Rikishi Kai has no collective bargaining powers, it does from time to time raise complaints with the association. These complaints are often taken under consideration but if nothing happens the wrestlers usually do not press further. At Rikishi Kai meetings, sekitori sometimes joke about going out on strike over something, but serious action is rarely contemplated if at all.

All 105 association oyakata have the right to own and operate their own stables, but very few are actually able to do so. One reason is the capital outlay, prohibitive for all but those highest ranking wrestlers who can attract very rich patrons, to buy land and erect a structure big enough to feed, house, and train a large group of wrestlers. Even when a new stablemaster (*shisho*) takes over an existing heya from a deceased or retired stablemaster, he usually must buy the stable itself as well as the right to assume its name. Another reason is the strong disapproval in the sumo world of stable proliferation, which is seen as a disruptive influence on the status quo. Only those wrestlers with exceptional power and prestige—and this usually means only the most successful yokozuna—are able to found their own stables upon retirement. At the end of 1972, there were only twenty-nine heya, some of them housing very few sumotori. Consequently only twenty-nine oyakata could serve as shisho; the rest usually join one of the various stables as coaches in addition to their other duties with the association. The number of heya changes from time to time due to the creation of new ones and, less frequently, the demise of old ones.

It might be added here that those men who do become stablemasters assume at least the fourth name of their lives. The first is their family name, the second the one they used in the ring, the third the toshiyori name they bought upon retirement, and the last the name of the stable. For men who changed their ring name once or more, the list is even longer.

A new heya is born in one of two ways. A new oyakata may build and head his own stable immediately after he retires from the ring. A recent example is ex-yokozuna Taiho, who retired in May 1971 after one of the most glorious careers in sumo history, with enough money and prestige to go out on his own. The other, and far more common, way is for an oyakata coach of an existing heya who has lost out in the power struggle to become the new stablemaster to leave and found his own heya, often taking some of the wrestlers with him. Such a move is not welcomed by sumo society because it weakens existing stables and can result in bad blood between certain oyakata, but the desire of all toshiyori to organize their own stable is a strong one.

If the break between an oyakata coach leaving a stable to form his own and the stablemaster of the existing heya is an amicable one, the new stable will maintain close ties with its parent heya. Such parent-child relationships between sumo stables are called *ichimon* (family, clan). Related stables often hold joint practice sessions and cooperate in other ways. The heya that Taiho founded belongs to the ichimon headed by the stable of which Taiho was a member during his wrestling days, Nishonoseki-beya. Nishonoseki-beya, in a pattern familiar to other large heya as well, also has in its family other stables which belong to men who either once wrestled for Nishonoseki itself or which are headed by men who broke away from the parent some time ago.

My stable, Takasago-beya, heads an ichimon comprised of three other stables, Wakamatsu-beya, Oyama-beya, and Kokonoe-beya. The stablemasters of Oyama and Wakamatsu are both second generation, their heya having been founded by their respective predecessors who both belonged to Takasago during their wrestling careers. The case of Kokonoe is different and is a good example of an unharmonious break between a parent and a new child. The Kokonoe stablemaster, the ex-yokozuna Chiyonoyama, wrestled for the Dewanoumi stable and became a coach there upon retirement. Seeing his hopes to become boss dashed when a younger man, the then yokozuna Sadanoyama, married the shisho's daughter and was named to succeed him, Chiyonoyama left to form his own heya. He took with him, among others, the stable's highest-ranking wrestler, ozeki Kitanofuji, who soon afterwards was promoted to yokozuna. Since Chiyonoyama's departure left great bitterness on both sides, there was no possibility for Kokonoe-beya to remain in the Dewanoumi ichimon. But being a smaller stable, Kokonoe needed to tie up with some large heya so the better wrestlers would get more opportunities to practice, among other reasons, and a deal was worked out for it to join the Takasago ichimon.

Wrestlers from the same ichimon used to be prohibited from facing each other in the ring. Perhaps it was thought to present too much potential danger of "family" friction among men on such intimate terms in their daily lives, or of "fixing" of matches if one "brother" needed a win at a certain basho more than another. But the relations between related stables are sometimes only nominal anyway, and the rule prevented contests between some of the strongest wrestlers. Consequently, it was changed in 1965. Today, only sumotori from the same heya are forbidden to wrestle each other in competition.

The purpose of the sumo heya is of course to train young wrestlers in the hopes of producing champions, and skillful recruitment is crucial. A stable which can boast of a great ozeki or yokozuna is likely to prosper because it can draw wealthy

patrons and the best apprentices. While a first-time spectator watching some of
the maku-uchi division giants work out might think that sumotori come from a
race apart, anyone who has seen the skinny boys in maezumo struggling to become
full-fledged wrestlers will agree that this is not so. Though usually larger than
most people, the teenage boys who enter sumo stables come from average Japanese families. The largest number hail from the more rugged, hard-working areas
of the nation such as the plains and mountains of Hokkaido, the snow country
of northern Honshu, and the fishing villages of Kyushu where nature and physical
labor combine to produce strong young bodies.

Successful recruitment depends ultimately on the support for and popularity
of sumo at the grass-roots level. Here, in the farming villages, the sport had its
origins in the shinji-zumo bouts which determined who held the divine will.
Though many young boys today prefer baseball and other modern sports, sumo
is still widely practiced in towns and villages throughout the country, and is an
organized sport in most schools and universities. Shrines in various areas feature
sumo bouts between youths at festivals held throughout the year. The youngest
sumotori are undoubtedly the one-year-old babies who compete every year in
"crying sumo," held on the eve of the beginning of spring in Hirado in Kyushu's
Nagasaki prefecture. Each young gladiator is held by a proud father dressed in
mawashi—the competitors are allowed to keep their diapers on in one of the few
breaches of sumo etiquette—and the first one to cry wins! Much older competitors
are the farmers near Sakai City in Nara Prefecture who stage a "muddy sumo"
contest every New Year's Day. Dressed in their work clothes, the fighters compete
in the fields. Unlike their professional counterparts, the farmer-sumotori do not
mind losing at all for it is believed that the muddier you become, the better the
crops and the healthier your family in the coming year. Countless other examples
could be cited; but such competitions as "muddy sumo," a direct descendent of
shinji-zumo, show very clearly the depth and tenacity of the sumo tradition in
the hearts of the Japanese.

On a more organized level are the student and amateur sumo groups. In elementary school, most boys practice a primitive form of sumo that is more like a
pushing and grappling game. In junior high, after a 1972 Ministry of Education
guideline, Japan's traditional sports of judo, kendo, and sumo have been elevated
from ten to twenty per cent of the physical education curriculum. High schools
and universities have sumo clubs which compete in annual national competitions
at which a yokozuna is crowned. Even adults are organized into amateur sumo
clubs that practice the sport as a part-time activity. Amateur sumo at all levels
comes under the auspices of the Nihon Sumo Renmei (Japan Sumo Federation)
which is the amateur equivalent of the Sumo Association. But a small percentage
of amateur competitors become professionals. Since most boys enter heyas soon
after junior high, and a pro's peak usually comes sometime in his middle to late
twenties, it would be very hard for an older recruit to compete. But there are
notable exceptions, especially from the universities.

Heya recruitment comes about in many ways. Stablemasters and coaches keep a keen eye out for talent as they tour the country for exhibitions and send out scouts if word-of-mouth reports of a strong youngster in a local area seem promising. Since most stables have support groups, patrons often suggest or introduce boys they know to the oyakata. Similarly, a certain stable may have strong ties with a particular region or prefecture—often because two or three of its oyakata or several of its wrestlers are natives of the area—and consequently receive help in local recruitment from various organizations there. And of course some boys eager to become sumotori approach a heya voluntarily and ask to be allowed to join.

Another smaller pool of talent is the university sumo club. Student champions sometimes decide to make sumo a career and are eagerly recruited by the stables. Two recent examples are the popular ex-collegians Wajima from Nippon University and Yutakayama (the former Nagahama) from Tokyo Agricultural University. Some university clubs form ties with certain stables. In the case of Wajima's university, the sumo club's dormitory and practice ring are directly behind Hanakago-beya in the Asagaya section of Tokyo and its members have the chance to work out with the stable's sumotori. When Wajima decided to turn pro, it was almost a foregone conclusion that he would wrestle for Hanakago. University graduates have the special privilege of skipping sumo's first three divisions and jumping directly into maku-shita for their first tournament in the big time. On the other hand, a college wrestler may be handicapped by the fact that he joins the heya some six or seven years later than his less-educated stablemates and so forfeits precious experience in the tougher world of professional training.

Recruits join a stable as junior high graduates at the age of fifteen or sixteen. The stablemaster provides the three basic necessities of life—food, clothing, and lodging—for all his charges (deshi), a fact that in the past led some poor parents to send their sons to sumo stables out of purely economic considerations. Stable bosses receive from the Sumo Association a set of allowances, separate from the salaries of the oyakata and sekitori wrestlers, to keep their heya in operation. The three basic allowances are earmarked for general stable maintenance, training-room upkeep, and raising wrestlers. The amount of each is calculated on the basis of one-man units, with more allowed for each wrestler in juryo and above than for each in maku-shita and below, and paid every two months. Stipends received from the association are augmented considerably by gifts from the heya koenkai (support groups) and individual patrons, but the amount varies greatly from stable to stable and is impossible to pin down.

Every new deshi, with the exception of those entering from a university, after participating in his first basho in maezumo and regardless of whether his results were good enough to elevate him to the lowest division at the next tourney, must attend the Sumo Kyoshujo (Sumo School). The school, located in Kokugikan in Tokyo, offers a six-month program which includes both physical exercise and classroom study. In the morning the students are taught basic sumo exercises, ceremonies, and practices by oyakata and older wrestlers from the various stables. In the afternoon, they receive from university teachers and other qualified instructors lessons in such subjects as sumo history, athletic medicine, physiology, sociology, Japanese, and calligraphy. What the new deshi learns at sumo school provides a core of knowledge which is then perfected during his first years in the heya. When I said all recruits go to sumo school after their first ring appearances in maezumo, I forgot to make one exception: myself. The reason I never went is simple. I couldn't speak, let alone read and write, Japanese when I arrived.

Life for the young, low-ranked deshi is, to put it mildly, laborious. They must get up at four or five every morning to clean up the training area and get in their practice before the upper-ranked wrestlers come to monopolize the ring sometime after 8:00. In the sumo stable, practice takes place once a day in the morning, and is usually over shortly after eleven. When their superiors arrive, the young deshi must stand around and watch, always at the ready to offer water to a perspiring sekitori or to tighten his mawashi. (Most heya have only one practice ring; my own Takasago-beya is fortunate in having two, so four sumotori can work out simultaneously.) The rest of the day is spent in endless chores: cooking and serving the meals; washing pots, pans, and clothes; cleaning the heya's many rooms; and running incessant errands for the oyakata and sekitori. Although the hours are longer and the job includes strenuous physical training, young sumotori are much like live-in servants who work for their room and board. There's one major difference, though: no days off. Believe me, it's rough. And it was even rougher when I first broke in than it is today.

IV

Chanko-nabe, Matawari and Bamboo sticks

Gaijin deshi

The first few weeks after I arrived in Japan were spent in Osaka getting ready for and wrestling in the March 1964 basho there. I was treated with respect and had it much easier than most new deshi. I slept in the same room with the two highest-ranking wrestlers in the stable, maegashira Fujinishiki and Maeda-gawa, and was allowed to eat and take a bath with the older wrestlers instead of waiting my turn like the youngest guys are supposed to. Everybody realized how strange everything was to me and tried to help me over the initial period as gently as possible. And Mrs. Takasago—whom the sports writers are fond of calling my "Japanese mama"—continued to supplement my diet with more familiar dishes. In Osaka I wrestled in maezumo and won eight straight pretty easily, which gave me the four points I needed to be on the banzuke in jo-no-kuchi for the following May tournament in Tokyo.

Except for the occasional light meals from Mrs. Takasago, the soft life ended when we returned to the stable in Tokyo. From then on I was treated like any other deshi of my low rank, which is bad enough without adding all the problems I had as a foreigner. The climate, which had bothered me most at first, seemed, suddenly, the least of my problems.

There was the very fundamental difficulty of communication. I could speak no Japanese and the wrestlers and coaches knew only the few words in English they remembered from school. Both Fujinishiki and Takasago gave me language books to study which listed English on one side and the corresponding Japanese on the other. When someone had a hard time getting across to me he'd point to a word or phrase in the books. But most of the wrestlers worked out more direct teaching methods for their new language student. They would grab my nose and say "*hana*," box my ears and yell "*mimi*," slap my hand, "*te*," or cup my eyes with their fingers, "*me*." Such methods made me catch on to simple con-structions pretty quickly, but it took much longer before I could hold any kind of conversation. Japanese is a helluva difficult language and still today I have problems.

More immediate than language, however, was my problem with the food. I found that I could stomach very little of the *chanko-nabe* which forms the basic diet of the sumotori. Chanko-nabe is a calorie-rich, highly nutritious stew eaten from a huge communal pot (*nabe*) together with great quantities of rice and ideal, apparently, for producing the large-bellied, heavy-hipped body crucial to

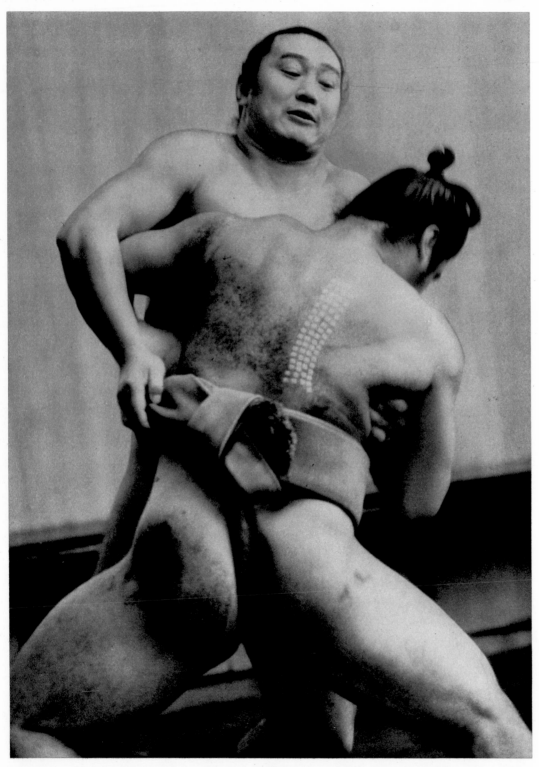

Training in the heya. Above, *two wrestlers have* hidari yotsu *(left-hand inside on the belt) and try to lift each other out. The wrestler with his back to the camera has small balm plasters on his back to help relax his muscles.* Right, *Jesse in his early days practicing the* taichiai. *(Baseball Magazine) Below, a typical practice session at Hanakago-beya.*

success in the sport. There are several varieties of chanko—beef, pork, chicken, or fish—but the basic ingredients include carrots, cabbage, onions, and bean curd simmered in a rich sauce of soy and sugar. Chanko-nabe is served at the two meals provided every day at the heya, one after practice at about 11:00 in the morning and one in the evening. People are often amazed that sumotori can get so big on only two meals a day, but the amounts of the rich food they can consume could hardly be called ordinary portions. Besides, higher-ranked wrestlers have the money to supplement their diet outside if they are still hungry or tired of the heya fare, and they are often treated to sumptuous feasts when they are entertained by patrons in the evening. Another thing I am sometimes asked is how wrestlers can train on an empty stomach every morning. It's actually not that hard to get used to. There is a theory that eating after a workout and then resting aids food digestion and absorption and helps one gain weight.

Although the taste of chanko was completely new to me, I was able to eat at least a bit of the meat varieties. But the fish chanko was served most often and it took me almost a year before I could stomach its strong smell and taste. Moreover, like everything else in the hierarchical world of sumo, the heya eats according to rank. The stablemaster and other oyakata sit down first, then the sekitori wrestlers, and so on down to the lowliest, who must wait until everyone else has had his fill and picked out all the choicest morsels. Things are better now, but then often the only thing left when we young guys got to eat was the soup at the bottom of the stew, plus rice. Takasago was really strict and told us if we wanted to eat well we'd just have to train hard and become sekitori wrestlers. The meals from Mrs. Takasago helped a lot in the beginning and later I was occasionally allowed to fry up some of the chanko ingredients such as vegetables or chicken in a way more to my liking, even though it was a breach of sumo discipline. And once in a while the lowest-ranking wrestlers would all chip in if we had a little cash and find something extra to cook.

The real hell came during *keiko* (training). I was stronger than probably anybody from the waist up, but weak—as all foreigners trying the sport are said to be—where it counts most in sumo, in the legs and hips. I was top-heavy in a world of heavy bottoms. Unlike the short-legged, strong-hipped Japanese wrestlers, whose bodies are more naturally suited for the sport partly, perhaps, from years of sitting and squatting on the floor, my long legs and high center of gravity made me extremely vulnerable to shorter wrestlers skilled in the various throwing techniques. My history of leg problems only made these exercises that bit more arduous. What the coaches tried to do essentially was "lower" my hips and strengthen my legs by putting me through an endless series of two of sumo's most basic exercises, *shiko* and *matawari*. Shiko, or stamping, involves raising each leg in turn as high as possible and bringing it down on the dirt with great force. Matawari, a stretching exercise and by far the most painful thing I was made to do, includes sitting on the ground and spreading the legs as wide as possible, ideally until they are almost perpendicular to the torso. A kind of sumo version of the split. From this rather unpleasant position the wrestler is then supposed to lean forward and touch his chest to the dirt. Since you're usually sweating profusely, dirt will cling to the chest if you're really getting down there all the way and the coaches can tell at a glance who's been dodging it and who hasn't. The pain of performing matawari was excruciating, but the oyakata were insistent. When I couldn't get my chest all the way to the ground a coach or older wrestler would stand behind me and lean heavily on my shoulders to force it the final few inches. Other exercises were designed for me personally. One was marching around the *keikoba* (training area) with one of the heaviest younger wrestlers on my shoulders and then doing deep knee bends similarly burdened. Another was dragging an automobile tire up a hill—with someone sitting in it.

Along with other exercises performed regularly such as rabbit-hopping around the keikoba and *teppo* (slamming the hands or pushing with all your might against wooden pillars), there was of course practice in actual fighting techniques. From the very beginning my opponents during keiko were always maku-shita wrestlers, even before I made the division myself at the end of 1964. This was because my size and strength put me more on a par with some of my stablemates in that division than smaller guys of equal rank with me. Also the coaches wanted to bring me along as fast as possible. To hasten my rise up the ladder and for other reasons I will explain shortly, I was made to concentrate exclusively on forcing my opponents out of the ring by pushing or thrusting. But to understand more clearly what I was and wasn't taught we should take a look at sumo technique.

Kimarite

I mentioned earlier the tsuridashi and utchari, two of the seventy winning techniques (*kimarite*) that have been officially listed by the Sumo Association. Some connoisseurs go as far as to claim there are actually over two hundred. To discuss them all would be hopelessly confusing, and take up far too much space. So let's concentrate on the most common ones, those the spectator is most likely to see at tournaments or in the heya keikoba.

Dividing sumo technique into two very broad categories, we can say there are two basic kinds of wrestlers: those who favor pushing or thrusting (*oshi-zumo*), which keep the opponent at arm's length; and those who employ some sort of grip on the opponent's mawashi (*yotsu-zumo*) or body, which leads to grappling, throwing, or tripping or a combination of all three. But, while wrestlers usually specialize in oshi-zumo or in one of the many belt grips or throws, the speed and rapidly changing nature of a sumo bout often forces the combatants to use several techniques within a few compact seconds. A man may maneuver his opponent to the rim with a belt grip and then switch to a push at the last moment just as his opponent, who has failed with his initial thrusting attack but feels himself suddenly free of his attacker's hold, will grab his mawashi in a last ditch utchari

Above right, *Jesse* practices matawari, *with someone behind to help, as coach Furiwake, now Takasago, looks on.* (Baseball Magazine) Below, *the positions reversed, Takamiyama helps a younger wrestler get right down.* Right, *Takamiyama practices* shiko—*with another wrestler on his back. Below right, mata-wari practice at Takasago-beya.*

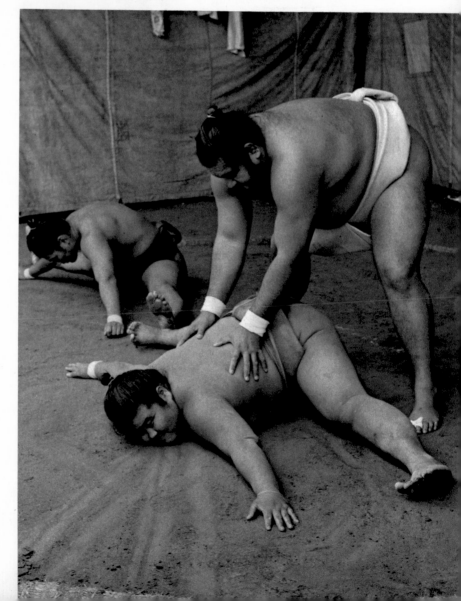

attempt. The variations are endless, and it is often only in slow-motion video replays that we realize how intricate the moves really were and what split-second timing was involved. The best wrestlers are quite naturally the well-rounded ones who match a strong fighting spirit with a varied technical arsenal.

For the follower who can recognize some of the techniques and knows what specialities to watch for as his favorite fighters ascend the ring, a trip to a basho becomes a much more interesting and rewarding experience.

Oshi-zumo: The techniques of oshi-zumo are divided into two groups, thrusts (*tsuki*) and pushes (*oshi*). Thrusting or slapping, called *tsuppari*, looks much like a high-speed boxing match except that the hands are open. (Clenched fists are illegal.) The base of each palm is thrust alternately against the opponent in piston-like fashion, the blows directed, most commonly at the chest or face, in an attempt to unbalance him and force him back out of the ring. Tsuppari exchanges produce some of the most violent and audible encounters in the sumo ring, especially when the face is slapped, and occasionally draw a bit of blood. Pushing, unlike tsuppari where the hand is repeatedly hitting the opponent's body, is a sustained thrust, with the palm or the hand (locked into a "v" formed by the thumb and the fingers) maintaining contact with the adversary. One of the most dramatic pushing attacks, difficult to shake off, is the *nodowa* (throat ring). The attacker locks his hand in the "v" position and pushes under the chin of his victim, often forcing his back to bend sharply like a bow. While grabbing the throat is an infraction leading to automatic defeat, the nodowa is a legal and frequently employed push. Sometimes the distinction between a thrust and a push is a fine one, but usually the difference is clear.

Thrusting techniques

Tsuki-dashi (thrust-out). A sustained tsuppari attack which forces the opponent out of the ring.

Tsuki-taoshi (thrust-down or slap-down). A tsuppari attack which fells the opponent, either inside or outside the ring.

Hataki-komi (slap-down onto all fours). Sidestepping a low charging opponent at the initial charge and, as he stumbles off balance, forcing him into the dirt with a whack on the back or neck.

Tsuki-otoshi (push-down from the side). This is a defensive technique used against an opponent who has gotten an arm inside, either on the belt or not. With a quick twist of the body and a thrust or push downward against his armpit or flank, the opponent is forced off balance. Sometimes only the opponent's hand touches the dirt. It is often impossible to tell whether the downward blow is a thrust or a push and this technique could just as well be classified under pushing techniques.

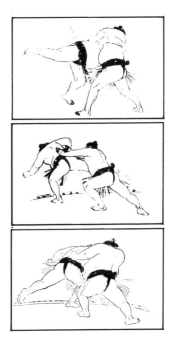

Okuri-dashi (thrust-out from the rear). One of the most embarrassing ways to lose, this occurs when a man gets turned around with his back momentarily to his opponent and is then thrust out.

Okuri-taoshi (thrust-out-and-down from the rear). The same as okuri-dashi except that the opponent falls.

Pushing Techniques

Oshi-dashi (push-out). Pushing an opponent out of the ring.

Oshi-taoshi (push-down). Toppling an opponent with a pushing attack, either inside or outside the ring.

Abise-taoshi (smother-down). Pushing with the chest against the chest of the opponent with arms outstretched. The whole body is used to push with the attacker almost riding on his victim's chest until he crumbles over backwards into the dirt.

Yotsu-zumo and the grapples, throws, and trips: These numerous techniques involve some kind of grip on the opponent's mawashi or body. Although oshi-zumo can often produce devastating, one-sided victories with the opponent being hurled out of the ring, a wrestler who relies solely on pushing or thrusting is at a disadvantage because his adversary always knows exactly what to expect and can plan his own defense accordingly. The greatest yokozuna have all been skilled beltmen. The two basic belt holds are the *yotsu* and the *uwate*. The yotsu is an inside belt grip with the arm inside the opponent's arm along his body. If the left arm is in this position it is called *hidari-yotsu*, if the right arm, *migi-yotsu*. Getting both hands inside on the belt is known as morozashi. The uwate is an outside belt hold secured by reaching around the opponent's arm (which would be in the yotsu position) or over his shoulder to grab his mawashi. The yotsu and uwate grips form the basis for many, but not all, of the forcing and throwing techniques. Some of the more common are:

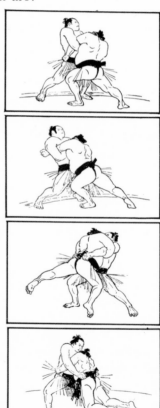

Yori-kiri (force-out). This is the most common winning technique in sumo. The aggressor forces the opponent to step outside the straw boundary by pushing with the body after securing a belt grip or getting an arm or arms under those of the loser.

Yori-taoshi (force-out-and-down). The same as yori-kiri except that the opponent is forced off his feet as he goes out of the ring.

Tsuri-dashi (lift-out). One of the most dramatic sights in the sport. The victim is literally lifted off his feet and deposited outside the ring, usually, but not always, after the aggressor has secured a moro-zashi. Execution of the tsuri-dashi requires great skill in getting both hands on the belt and tremendous strength in lifting out.

Tsuri-otoshi (lift-and-force-down). If the opponent's struggling prevents lifting him out, he can be forced down onto his knees by using the belt holds to apply downward pressure.

Uwate-nage (outside arm throw). Securing an uwate hold with either the left or right hand, the winner twists his hip under the opponent and leans forward, throwing him down. A similar vari-

ation is called *uwatedashi-nage* in which the hold
on the mawashi is at the opponent's side. The attacker puts his head on the loser's shoulder and,
turning his body to the side, uses a sharp wrist
throw to topple him. Sometimes the only clear
difference between these two techniques is that the
wrestlers are much closer together during uwate-
nage, which makes more use of the power in arm
and body, than in uwatedashi-nage where the
bodies are farther apart and power comes from the
wrist.

Kote-nage (forearm throw). An outside arm throw
similar in principle to uwate-nage except that the
mawashi is not used. Kote-nage is executed by
grasping the opponent's back or curling the arm
around his inside arm and throwing him down.

Shitate-nage (inside arm throw). An inside belt
grip is used to twist the opponent and throw him.
A variation, *shitatedashi-nage*, is similar to the
uwate-dashi-nage except that it is performed from
an inside belt hold.

Sukui-nage (scoop throw). An inside arm throw
similar to shitate-nage except that the mawashi is
not grabbed, as in kote-nage. The inner arm is
wrapped around the opponent's shoulder and the
hip is shifted under his body from which position
the twisting throw is unleashed.

Kubi-nage (neck throw). The victor wraps his
arm around the opponent's neck and twists him
into the dirt. Kubi-nage is usually a throw at-
tempted in desperation such as when the opponent
has secured a morozashi.

Tottari (arm-twist). This throw is usually employed when an opening is seen during a pushing
or thrusting encounter. From the right side, the
opponent's right arm is taken with both arms, the
left hand holding the wrist, the right arm curled
under the elbow. By leaning forward and twisting
the arm, the victor throws his opponent off balance into the dirt.

Uchi-gake (inside leg spill). The victor winds his leg from the inside around the back of his opponent's leg after gripping his belt. The loser is then quickly toppled.

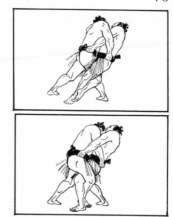

Soto-gake (outside leg spill). Similar to uchi-gake except that the aggressor's leg is wrapped around the back of the opponent's leg from the outside.

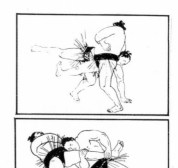

Ketaguri (kick and pull). At the initial charge, the winner kicks one of his opponent's legs out from under him, and at the same instant applies the coup de grace by pulling his arm forward or whacking him on the shoulder. Ketaguri is frequently used by a fast, little man to trip up a big man before he has a chance to get started.

Ashi-tori (leg throw). An uncommon but interesting throw. The attacker grabs the victim's leg with both hands, his right arm curled around the calf, his left grasping the ankle, and topples him over backwards.

Utchari (backward pivot throw). This is the spectacular and crowd-pleasing throw which turns apparent defeat into sudden victory. The seemingly sure loser makes a heroic last ditch stand at the straw rim, finally lifting the aggressor off his feet and swinging him around the body and out. The loser's foot touches out a second before both men crash into the crowd.

The above list describes only twenty-six of the seventy techniques, but it includes the most common and gives an idea of the great variety and complexity of maneuvers that fill the short minutes of a sumo bout. While the purpose of battle is a simple one, ousting or downing the opponent can require seemingly infinite combinations of skills.

There are a few terms outside those used to describe the official winning tactics which nonetheless have a bearing on victory and defeat. Fouls (*hansoku*), lead to automatic defeat. It is very rarely that a wrestler loses by breaking a rule. When infractions do occur they are usually unintentional, such as when an attacker gets his fingers caught in his opponent's topknot and finds himself dragging his man down by the hair. Two more common occurrences, *isami-ashi* and *okuri-ashi*, are often confusing. Isami-ashi is used to describe the action of a wrestler who, on the verge of sure victory by forcing, thrusting, or pushing his victim out, carelessly steps beyond the circle before his opponent in an impetuous desire to finish him off. As in the case of hansoku, the wrestler has not been beaten; he has beaten himself. Okuri-ashi refers to the leg of a sumotori performing the lift-out (tsuri-dashi), and seems to contradict the basic rule of sumo that the man who touches outside the circle first is the loser. If the attacker has lifted his opponent off his feet and carried him over the boundary so that his body is completely out of the ring although still airborn, he is allowed to step outside the ring himself before depositing the loser on the ground. Thus the winner has touched out before the loser, but the victory is nevertheless clear-cut and convincing.

One of the most controversial and least-understood decisions in sumo involves an infrequent occurrence known as *kabaite*, a curious exception to the hard-and-fast rule that the man who touches down first (*tsukite*) with any part of his body is the loser. When two sumotori fall in the ring at the same instant with one man directly over the other, there is a good possibility of serious injury to the man on the bottom. In such a situation, the wrestler on top may extend his hand to break his fall and protect his opponent from the full weight of his descending body. Even though his hand touched the dirt before any part of the man under him, his act was a conscious consideration for his opponent's health and he is declared the winner. For had he not put out his hand, the body of the man crushed beneath him would naturally have hit the ground first. The problem is not with the rule itself, a remarkable example of sumo manners and good-sportsmanship extending to the very heat of battle itself, but rather with the extreme difficulty in determining whether the kabaite was an intentional act of mercy or not and whether the two bodies were really about to fall so as to cause serious injury. A recent example occurred in the 1972 January tournament during the last bout of the eighth day between yokozuna Kitanofuji and sekiwake Takanohana. The referee gave the victory to Takanohana (who was on the bottom), claiming that it was a case of tsukite. But the five judges— oyakata who have the right to overrule the referee—held a conference and decided that it was a case of kabaite, awarding the victory to Kitanofuji. Opponents of the decision claimed that pictures showed very clearly that Takanohana was twisting Kitanofuji to the side as they fell and thus the yokozuna would have landed to his side, not on top of him. Defenders staunchly insisted that the case was a clear kabaite. Kitanofuji said that of course it was kabaite. Takanohana said nothing. But the referee was made to sit out the rest of the basho— although this one decision was not the only reason—and quit soon after. Most referees today probably pray that they will never have to face a similar situation.

When it came time for me to learn technique in the Takasago-beya ring, I was told one thing: push. Push, push, push was all I heard, and everyone even

There is time for a little relaxation after the day's training.

knew the English word. I was told to forget about beltwork and concentrate on
tsuppari and pushing. If I went for the belt during my first year I was hit on the
back and told to keep pushing, and even during the second I was scolded for
grabbing the mawashi. The reasons were several. For someone built as I was,
with a strong upper body and powerful arms but weak underpinnings and a
high charge, the most effective tactic was to try to thrust or push my opponent
out. Coming to grips on the belt would neutralize my pushing power and enhance
the likelihood of my being thrown off balance, since my waist was weak and I
had a hard time keeping my footing when forced or twisted sideways. The
coaches also felt that my push was a great natural weapon which should be
developed as much as possible. One even claimed that it had the same destructive
power as that of former yokozuna Chiyonoyama, a noted oshi-zumo artist.
Another reason was the belief that I would rise faster up the ranks through
pushing. If two wrestlers trained for three years, one concentrating on beltwork,
the other on the oshi techniques, the pusher is likely to advance faster. I don't
know whether the beltman would rise higher in the end, but this of course
depends on other factors as well as technique. Since I joined the heya at nineteen,
older than most of the my stablemates, they probably wanted to give me the
technique that would allow me to go up the quickest. I should add that later,
toward the end of my second year at the heya, my instructors began to show
me how to grab the belt, but mostly in order to steady myself while executing
techniques like yori-kiri or tsuri-dashi. Even today, I only rarely try one of the
throws.

A third reason for the emphasis on oshi-zumo at Takasago-beya was tradition.
It is a common custom for a deshi to be taught the technique that was used by
his shisho during his wrestling career. The tradition of oshi-zumo at Takasago-
beya began in the Taisho Period (1912–1925) with ozeki Tachihikari, and has
persisted, although there were periods when yotsu-zumo was emphasized·as well,
such as under the third Takasago, the former ozeki Asashio. Both the stablemaster who brought me from Hawaii, the fourth Takasago (former yokozuna
Maedayama) and the coach most directly responsible for my training, Furiwake
(the former yokozuna Asashio who became the fifth Takasago on the death of
his predecessor in August 1971) were specialists in oshi-zumo. It was natural
that I, like many of my stablemates, would be led to practice tsuppari and the
other oshi techniques. Fujizakura and Maenoyama, who join me in representing
the stable in the top division, are both skilled practitioners of oshi-zumo.

Kawaigatte and the ani-deshi

Let me describe an average day during my first and roughest year in the stable.
It is probably more or less typical of what all young deshi go through, except
for the added difficulties I had as a foreigner. I used to get up about 4:30,
because we had to be in the keikoba by 5 to begin working out. We were actually
awakened by the *wakamono gashira*, usually a retired wrestler who never made

sekitori who stays on at the heya to manage the younger wrestlers and to perform other duties both at the stable and during tournaments. Practice began with exercises like shiko, matawari, and teppo to loosen up and work up a sweat. Then we started training in the ring. First we would join in *moshiai*, a kind of king-of-the-mountain elimination where the winner stays in to take on the next comer. Then I'd fight a long series of bouts against the same opponent (*sanban*). Coach Furiwake and some of the older maku-shita wrestlers really pushed me, forced me to keep going, often giving me a good whack with the end of a broomstick. I learned later that the wrestlers who get pushed the hardest in training by the coaches are the ones who are seen to have the most potential; older maku-shita wrestlers or even sekitori who have passed their peak and have little chance of going much higher are left pretty much alone. But I really wondered at the time why they were bearing down so hard on me.

After finishing one sanban series, I had to take on a new opponent for another round. Ringwork ended with a grueling drill called *butsukari-geiko*, which involves running against another sumotori with full force and trying to push him across the ring while he digs his heels into the dirt and leans forward in resistance. The resister tries to totally exhaust the attacker by alternating his response to each charge: he may stand firm and allow himself to be pushed back slowly inch by inch; flip his opponent to the ground with a judo-like throw (an all-important drill which teaches a wrestler how to fall and avoid injury when he and his opponent crash off the raised tournament dohyo together); or grab the back of the neck and force his man to walk around the ring in a squatting position. Every wrestler does butsukari-geiko after finishing his workout in the ring and then "gives his chest" (*mune dasu*) to one or more of his stablemates in the role of resister. The exercise is an important one, but always leaves you completely winded. What made it really bad was that a few older maku-shita wrestlers often hit me on the back or legs with bamboo sticks as I was performing butsukari-geiko. They would even spit at us sometimes or throw salt into our mouths. Since they were our seniors there was nothing we could do in return, but I was sometimes boiling inside.

Hitting or roughing up a young guy in sumo, much commoner when I began than it is today, is referred to as *kawaigatte*, from the verb *kawaigaru* which means to treat with love and affection. That the sumo world should turn the meaning of the word upside down is not really as contradictory as it may seem at first glance and is an excellent example of the philosophy behind so much of heya life. Although there can be exceptions in any stable, an oyakata, or senior wrestler does not hit a young deshi just to be mean or because he dislikes him. The purpose—except when punishment is involved—is to make him angry, and fan the flames of his fighting spirit; to force him to give his all by pushing himself beyond what he thinks he can take; to build his desire to become a sekitori, and, if possible, a yokozuna. It is a form of encouragement, if rather a strict one, which demonstrates concern, not malice. Viewed in this light, the use of the word kawaigatte becomes less curious. Kawaigatte, like keiko itself, the stress on manners, etiquette, and all those other though aspects of heya life is meant to build the unique spirit that alone can produce good wrestlers and good men. All of this took some time to dawn on me as I realize now, looking back from the relative comfort of secure sekitori status.

Although thoroughly worn out from butsukari-geiko, I was not through yet. I had to follow up ringwork with more exercises, shiko again, and matawari. Maybe I needed it more, but I really felt I was going about three times harder than everyone else. I did so many shiko every day—it must have been close to five hundred—that my legs were so sore I could hardly walk and my whole body was stiff and aching. I began losing weight instead of gaining my first year, a rather strange situation for a sumotori and one my problems with the food did little to alleviate. I kept telling myself you can take it, you can take it, but there were times when I seriously wondered. I remember more than once in the training area feeling tears come to my eyes after being hit. They asked me if I was crying and I said: "No, that's sweat. I'm not crying, I'm sweating." There were many days when I was genuinely afraid to go into the keikoba.

After working out steadily for almost two hours, sometimes closer to three, I stood around with the other younger wrestlers watching the sekitori train. We all held towels which we used to wipe sweat or dirt from the faces and chests of the sekitori and were constantly making trips to the water bucket to give them drinks or making sure that their mawashi stayed good and tight. We had to be ready to perform any service that they might ask for, from applying a bandage to retying a fallen topknot. When practice ended sometime after eleven, the oyakata and sekitori took baths, and each apprentice had to help the man to whom he was personally assigned as tsukebito (attendant) wash himself. I was one of Takasago's tsukebito during most of my three pre-sekitori years, and since the stablemaster always goes first, I had to be ready to get into the bathroom quickly on those days when he decided to bathe with the wrestlers.

When the oyakata and sekitori had finished their ablutions, they sat down to the morning meal. The apprentices took turns preparing and cooking the chanko-nabe, a mess detail called *chanko-ban*. On the days when they were cooking, deshi left the keikoba after their own early workouts. Cooking was one of the few heya duties I was spared. Since I had trouble enough eating Japanese cuisine let alone attempting to prepare it, the oyakata wisely reasoned that everyone's stomachs would be far better off if I was kept out of the kitchen, at least until it came time for dishwashing. But I did help serve. We stood around the steaming pot, gargantuan, semi-nude waiters, adding fresh ingredients to the simmering stew, filling empty rice bowls, bringing cold drinks, and clearing dirty dishes. Only after everyone else had finished and retired for an afternoon nap were we able to sit down and eat what was left and then take a bath.

During the afternoon, if I was on chanko-ban, I had to wash pots and pans. Otherwise my duties would include putting away bedding and tidying up the sekitori wrestlers' rooms after they had finished their siesta; also laundry, cleaning the toilet, and sweeping the dining room in preparation for the second and final meal of the day served between five and six. And there were constant errands to run for the oyakata and sekitori. I wasn't allowed to sleep until evening. The older maku-shita wrestlers told the apprentices that we were still too lowly to have the right to sleep, and if one of them caught us napping he would leave us sore for a week. We all particularly dreaded doing something wrong in front of the stablemaster and tried to stay as far away from him as possible. Takasago was very strict. Once he tore into me after he caught me grumbling to another wrestler: "Jesse, if you can't take it, go back home." I shut up fast. But he had, at the same time, a tremendous amount of what the Japanese call *kanroku,* dignity. It was an awesome combination. I remember when he watched us in the keikoba he never said very much, and it was coach Furiwake and others who were most respon-sible for training me personally. But his mere presence created an intensified atmosphere that made everyone really get down to work. We seemed to know what we had to do just by looking at him. In a quiet way, he was the one who taught me the most about mental discipline.

After serving the evening meal and cleaning up, there was usually some final chore such as washing clothes. And often we had to get a sekitori ready to go out by helping him into his kimono and running out to find a taxi. Each long and exhausting day ended about eight or nine when I finally got to lie down and close my eyes.

It was a group of older wrestlers in the maku-shita division who gave the apprentices the hardest time. Today we have only about twenty-five men in my stable, but then the heya was much bigger with about sixty sumotori. And there was a large group of maku-shita guys between the ages of twenty-eight and thirty who had either never been sekitori at all or who had been up in the juryo division for one or two tournaments and fallen back down. Some of them had been in the stable for over twelve years and had great seniority in years if not in rank. We referred to them as *ani-deshi* (older brother deshi). Since all wrestlers in the stable are deshi of the oyakata, ani-deshi literally refers to any stablemate, sekitori included, who has more heya seniority than yourself, regardless of rank. The opposite term is *ototo-deshi* or younger brother deshi. But since sekitori wrestlers in the two top divisions have a rank status that transcends age in the heya pecking order, I usually thought of the oldest non-sekitori wrestlers when I used the term ani-deshi. Because of busy schedules and more elevated status, the oyakata and sekitori wrestlers could rarely afford much time to instruct the younger boys in the routine of heya life. This job was entrusted largely to the ani-deshi wrestlers in maku-shita, who also taught us a lot of the basic exercises and techniques in the keikoba before the sekitori arrived to practice every morn-ing. In any heya, knowledge is handed down from the older to the younger much like clothes in a large family. Everyone with seniority has to do some teaching, and the busy oyakata rely heavily on experienced wrestlers below the juryo

Overleaf, bath time. Takamiyama gets a rubdown from one of his tsukebito. ▶

division who are around most of the time. It was with this group of maku-shita stablemates that I had the most day-to-day contact.

Although invaluable as teachers, certain maku-shita ani-deshi, with long years of service in the sport but little prospect of advancing to juryo or maku-uchi, occasionally took out their frustrations on their young subordinates. Coming in from a long night of drinking, they would sometimes wake up the apprentices and force them to do needless chores or knock them around a bit. Or, when discipline was demanded, they might perform with a broom or bamboo stick more enthusiastically than the situation called for. It was also wrestlers from this group who were responsible for most of the whacks with bamboo sticks we received during butsukari-geiko. Things now are very different. There are few beatings and when a senior does take a broom handle to a young wrestler in the keikoba it is usually at least half in jest.

During those first two most difficult years I was usually accompanied by an ani-deshi when I went out because of my language problem, and I could never go out alone without getting permission from one of them. I slept in a room with five maku-shita wrestlers. I usually went to sleep early, but some of my roommates often went out in the evenings and came back very late. Since this was when they became most rambunctious, I always dreaded their return and lay there shaking on my futon. But though some apprentices had a rough time of it, I was only beaten, except in rare cases, when I did something wrong and in the training area. I was able to avoid more arbitrary treatment largely because I had gained the respect of my superiors. This respect was earned perhaps because I was obviously struggling very hard to overcome the many handicaps I faced, but I think, too, that my general attitude had a lot to do with it. I didn't complain and when I was told to do something I would quickly say "*hai*" (yes) and run. I kept my gripes, and serious doubts about my decision to enter the sumo world in the first place largely to myself. And my swift rise through the first three divisions helped. By the end of my first year I had entered the bottom of the maku-shita division and was roughly equal in rank, if not in seniority, with many of the ani-deshi.

I did not escape humiliation altogether, however. In April 1965, when we were returning to Tokyo from an exhibition tournament in Hiroshima, I was slapped hard across the face by a fellow maku-shita wrestler because I had failed to get his permission to go out on one occasion. It wasn't the blow that bothered me so much as the fact that he did it in front of all the other wrestlers and the crowd of onlookers that sumotori always draw when they travel in groups. A more serious incident took place during an exhibition tour of the island of Shikoku in October of 1966. I was at that time serving in a group of tsukebito assigned to Takasago. One of the tsukebito forgot the boss's hat at a train station, and although Takasago never found out, a group of ani-deshi wrestlers decided to make sure such a thing didn't happen again. They gathered all the wrestlers serving Takasago in a schoolyard and put us through butsukari-geiko. When we started to tire and drag they hit us on the backs with boards. Since I wasn't directly responsible, I escaped with only a light beating, but the guy who forgot the hat got a hell of a one. He had bruises all over his back.

Such treatment made me seethe inside but I just had to grin and bear it. I didn't mind so much being hit occasionally in the keikoba or being given a rough time when I'd done something wrong, but being beaten or picked on unfairly was hard to stomach in silence. And it was not only physical punishment that could get out of hand. Certain sekitori wrestlers took advantage of their rank to make unreasonable demands on younger wrestlers. They would call a man from another room to turn on the television set right next to them or make someone massage them for two or three straight hours while they slept. Looking back now, with a wider and more sober perspective, I realize that a certain amount of razzing is necessary as long as it doesn't become extreme. Young guys don't learn much unless demands are made and sometimes you really have to rub on them. I've learned because I've seen a lot of young sumotori. They get tired, and if you don't scold them and hound them they'll just slack off. Many, of course, can't take it. I'd say that for every ten boys who try to become sumotori, six will run away. Since I became a sekitori, I've tried to be fair, but I don't have a reputation in the heya for always being a nice guy.

I don't know how many times I decided to quit during those first two years. Sumo's tests of mental and physical endurance were bad enough even without all the aspects of Japanese life that I wasn't used to. Although I tried not to let my emotions show when I was around the oyakata and other wrestlers, my pillow was often damp on those nights when I wasn't exhausted enough to fall right to sleep. I even wrote home at one point asking for money for the return trip, but people there told me to stick it out, and members of the Maui Sumo Association tried to encourage me with mail and visits when they came to Japan. One day, wanting to be alone but with nowhere to escape to, I boarded a train on Tokyo's Yamanote Line which encloses the city's main downtown areas in a huge loop. Circling round and round for over two hours, I pondered what to do, changing my mind over and over again. But even had I decided to try to leave, it would have been almost impossible to return to Hawaii. I had no money and was completely dependent on the stable boss. Before coming to Japan, I had made a five-year contract with Takasago which provided for my transportation to Tokyo and my maintenance at the heya. He had agreed to pay for my return home if I failed to become a sekitori within the five years, but not before. Besides, I didn't even have my passport. Mrs. Takasago, who handled most of my official affairs, was holding it for safe-keeping. I don't really feel that she locked it up to prevent me from leaving, but on the other hand I doubt whether I could have had it on demand.

Many friends in both Japan and the United States seem to marvel at what they refer to as my ability to triumph against almost overwhelming odds, and one of the questions I am constantly asked is how I stuck it out. The best word

Everyday the wrestlers long hair must be combed out, oiled, and tied into the traditional hair style. Below, *a short sleep on a futon in the early afternoon. Above left, three* tsukebito massage a sekitori—*one of his many privileges. Below left, the* sekitori *wrestlers sit down to a lunch of* chanko-nabe, *while the younger wrestlers act as waiters.*

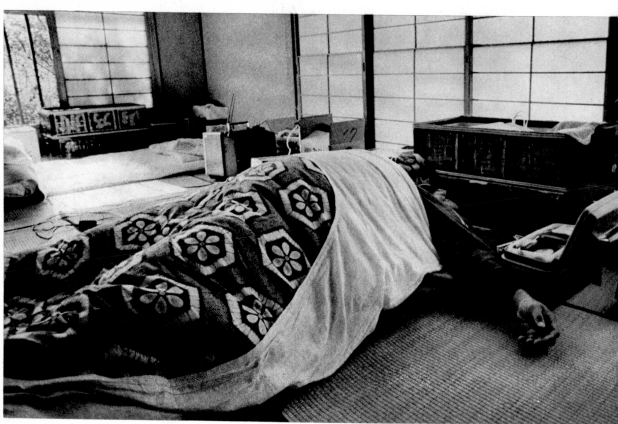

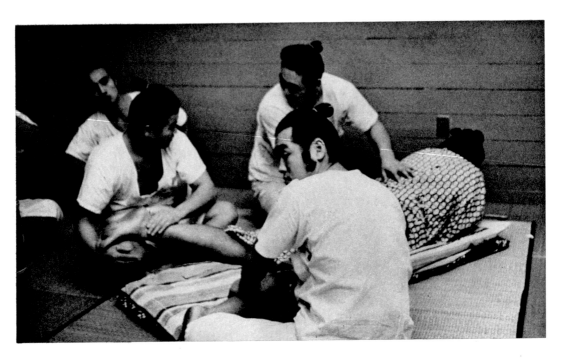

I can think of to describe how I got through the first couple of years is *gaman* (forbearance, endurance). Long before I learned the Japanese term, from around the time I was still in grade school, I had known the feeling and had been able to handle trouble. There were other reasons why I couldn't let myself give up. When I was invited to Japan by Takasago I knew that this was my chance, perhaps my only one, to really be something. After I got here I was pushed, really forced, in training and this got me mad inside. It made me want to prove that I could do it, that I had the will. But perhaps what helped me most of all were the people who had faith in me and encouraged me, from Takasago and my stablemates to countless friends in Hawaii and Japan. I couldn't let them down. And I felt that I could help make sumo more popular in the United States and maybe beyond. If I'd quit, it would have been bad not only for me but for what the sumo world thinks of foreigners in general, and I might have hurt the chances of another non-Japanese wanting to give sumo a try.

Of course this is all easy to say now. I wasn't exactly thinking about the international repercussions of my presence or lack of it in Takasago-beya when Coach Furiwake was ordering me to do one hundred, only one hundred, more shiko at the end of a day's workout. I was sometimes so sore it hurt even to lie down, and I could think only of airplanes leaving Tokyo and palm trees.

Along with the minor aches and pains, my daily battles in the keikoba left more permanent scars. During the late summer of 1964, my left ear, constantly slapped and cuffed in training, began to hurt, eventually causing so much discomfort that I couldn't sleep on my left side for about a month. I asked the coaches for a couple of days off, but got only a terse refusal: "*Bakayaro*! (You idiot!) Train harder!" Gradually, after applying heat to the ear on a doctor's recommendation, the pain subsided. But it was not until four months later that I saw the extent of the damage; after my hair had finally grown long enough it was put into the characteristic topknot (*chon-mage*) of the sumotori—said to be worn for the purpose of tensing the body for combat, unifying power from head to toe, and to help prevent head injury in case of a fall—and in my case revealed that I had acquired a full-blown cauliflower ear, a common occupational hazard of the sport and in one sense a kind of badge of acceptance into the sumo fraternity.

More serious was the injury to my throat two years after I arrived in Japan. My tonsils had been giving me trouble from the beginning due to the cold, damp winters, and I finally had them removed in January of 1966. After the operation I took two weeks off from training, but my throat was still tender as I began to get ready for the Osaka basho that March. In the last bout of ringwork one day, just as my opponent and I were about to charge, I raised my hand, the indication that you are not ready, and began to straighten up prior to reassuming the charging crouch. Unluckily, he either did not see the signal or thought I was charging and rammed into me. Unprepared and off balance, I was hit hard in the throat. The accident injured my left vocal chord, leaving my speaking voice little more than a husky whisper. Doctors told me that an operation requiring between six months and a year away from the sumo ring was needed to repair the damage, but since resting meant demotion, I chose to wait until I retire to undergo surgery. I was advancing in the maku-shita division with my sights set on juryo and sekitori status. Staying out of some four consecutive basho would have meant four demotions way back down the ladder. The doctor said that, short of an operation, I could at least spare my voice by writing down what I wanted to say. But I like to talk and I couldn't write Japanese anyway. If I do talk too much, I occasionally lose my voice for short periods.

My tribulations at Takasago-beya were not, however, without their lighter side. My stablemates still get a great kick out of imitating my early attempts to speak Japanese. Asaarashi loves to tell of the way I often mixed the two languages. "Jesse used to add the English word 'man' to the end of most of his sentences. You, know, like 'umai man' ('that's delicious, man') or 'bikkuri shita man' ('I was surprised, man'). We thought at first that 'man' was some mispronounced Japanese word and tried to figure out what he was trying to say. But when we found out it was English we began to dig it and even use it ourselves. Jesse doesn't use it at all anymore when he's speaking in Japanese, but we still do now and again." I made the most out of the English words that my stablemates did know, like "tomorrow." Simply by repeating the word in succession I could express the idea of the day after tomorrow long before I'd mastered the appropriate Japanese word. Similarly, "tomorrow tomorrow tomorrow iku" got across the idea of going somewhere in three days and only required one simple Japanese word, "iku," to go.

My unfamiliarity with certain customs also gave the boys a good chance to have a laugh at my expense. One particularly embarrassing episode was my first classic encounter with a Japanese bath. It was in Osaka soon after I first arrived from Hawaii. Sumotori live in temples during tournaments away from Tokyo, and if there is no big bath there we use a nearby public bath. We usually rent the whole place for a couple of hours each morning after practice. Japanese custom requires washing outside the communal tub, rinsing thoroughly, and then climbing in to soak. I either forgot what I had been told or didn't understand because I jumped right in with soap all over my body. Asaarashi and the others were shocked and yelled at me in the only English they knew: "Oh, no, no. Jesse, Jesse, no, no, no."

Later I was able to have a laugh of my own. During the summer of 1965 the old heya building was torn down and the present concrete structure erected. The new stable incorporated many sensible ideas such as two practice rings which allowed more wrestlers to work out at the same time. And the more modern facilities included Western-style toilets, more comfortable for the large bodies of sumotori than the squatting Japanese-style ones we had in the old building. Just after the building was completed we got a new recruit from a remote rural area of the country. Confused at facing such an alien contraption for the first time, the boy pondered for a moment and then climbed up on top of the bowl to use it in Japanese fashion. It was now my turn to protest "no, no, no."

Despite the strangeness of my presence in one of the least cosmopolitan communities in existence, I was remarkably well-accepted in the sumo world in general and particularly in my own heya. I know some people in sumo society thought Takasago was crazy to try to bring an American into his stable and there are probably some purists who resented opening the doors of Japan's national sport to foreigners. But I never really felt much prejudice. Takasago warned me when I first arrived that in the closed world of sumo I would have to expect that some wrestlers in other stables would not want to lose to a foreigner and would go all out against me in the ring, but that I should ignore such feelings, work hard in the keikoba to become a high-ranking sekitori and let my deeds speak for themselves. I don't think very many wrestlers felt this way and, besides, what sumotori wants to lose to anyone, foreigner or not? At Takasago itself, there was a bit of faint hostility at the very outset, mostly because of some of the special treatment I received, such as the meals from Mrs. Takasago. But this quickly disappeared because I think most of my stablemates realized the unique problems I faced and respected the way I put out. Asaarashi and I went out together a lot during my first two years and he knows me perhaps the best of my stablemates today. I was once really embarrassed, but rather proud, to overhear him talking about those early days with a friend: "Some of us were a bit envious of the special treatment Jesse got, especially from Mrs. Takasago. But we realized the reasons for it, and what he was up against here as a foreigner. Jesse's genuineness and heart impressed us all and soon won him our acceptance and friendship. And the way he trained was something else. We all had to bow our heads in respect." If Asaarashi retires before I do, I think I'll hire him to write my press releases.

V

Maezumo through Maku-shita

Butterflies, championships, and tears

The way I blitzed through the first three divisions made me wonder why the hell I had to train so hard. As I mentioned before, at my first tournament appearance in Osaka in March 1964 I quickly won the eight straight bouts I needed in maezumo to be officially ranked in the lowest division for the following basho in May. In maezumo I wrestled under my own first name, Jesse, but after I qualified for the banzuke, Takasago honored me with one of the stable's most prestigious wrestling names: Daigoro Takamiyama, the Meiji-period reformer who had founded Takasago-beya. The name Takamiyama, which means "mountain of the lofty view," was originally taken from a 1,249-meter peak which stands on the border between Japan's Nara and Mie prefectures. I was not fully aware of the honor Takasago had bestowed on me, however, until later. It was exciting to get a sumo name, but my knowledge of sumo was almost nonexistent and all I really understood was that the name was a good one. I didn't know its history or real significance until I got back to Tokyo in May.

In the Tokyo basho that May I tied two other wrestlers in the jo-no-kuchi division with a 6–1 record and then won a three-way playoff to capture the division championship. This meant that I would move directly into the next division up, jo-nidan, for the tournament in Nagoya in July. During my jo-no-kuchi basho something happened that I still chuckle about. My opponent in one of the bouts was a guy who was as tall as I was but real skinny. He must have been afraid of me because instead of charging at the tachiai he ran away back to the edge of the ring. If a wrestler is not quite ready when the referee says it's time he will signal his opponent by raising his hand and saying "*matta*," and the two fighters will straighten up momentarily before crouching again for the charge. But this guy just turned his back and ran. I was only twice his weight, so why should he have been scared of me? The referee did get us together again at the center of the ring, however, and we finally had a tachiai. I pushed him out easily, but the whole thing was quite a surprise.

Two months later in Nagoya I had a perfect 7–0 record in jo-nidan and beat the only other undefeated man in a playoff to win my second straight division title. This guaranteed a jump to a fairly high position in the division above, sandanme, for the Tokyo basho in September. Although I lost two bouts in Tokyo, my 5–2 record was good enough to secure entry into the bottom of

maku-shita for the November Kyushu tournament. So after only four basho and less than a year in Japan, I was only one division away from juryo and becoming a sekitori. It's funny that though I was winning consistently, I was very nervous before fights. On nights before bouts I always had awful butterflies and couldn't sleep. I finally got used to it around the time of the Kyushu tournament that first year, and the butterflies began to subside. It's too bad, because I could have used them.

Although I was 5–2 in Kyushu during my first appearance in maku-shita, the tougher competition in that division soon burst my winning bubble and taught me that the climb to the top was going to be a long and rough one. I was to spend the next two years sliding up and down the maku-shita ladder.

I cried after my first losing tournament, the New Year's basho in Tokyo in January 1965. Though I finally looked like a real sumotori because I had grown enough hair to have it fixed in a chon-mage, I sure didn't feel like I should be one. My 2–5 record seemed to confirm my deepest doubts, and I felt sick inside, certain that I had made the wrong move in coming to Japan. This was the time that I wrote home asking for money. I guess all the problems I was having adapting to Japan and heya life came to a head. It was certainly one of the darkest moments in my career. It was also the time I was down to my lowest weight. I had been losing almost steadily since my arrival and hit bottom at about 205, over 150 pounds less than I weigh now. I really wanted to go home.

Takasago and the coaches had a different solution for my problems: stiffer training. They said my size had made the difference against the smaller boys in the lower divisions, but from here on I would have to hone my pushing and thrusting techniques learn to get my butt down lower at the charge, and learn how to counter the skilled beltmen. I was still weak in the hips and often lost my balance, so coach Furiwake and some older wrestlers such as Hibikiya intensified my shiko and matawari routines. Takasago occasionally directed my exercises but even when he didn't he was always there in the keikoba, watching. He told me that losing doesn't matter, that the important thing is giving one hundred per cent all the time in training and being able to make the opponent fight your fight. If a wrestler can do that, victories will come as a matter of course. Most of all, the boss taught me what spirit and guts were all about, and it is to him that I owe the most for my eventual success.

The anniversary of my first appearance in the professional sumo ring, the Osaka basho in March 1965, was a bright one. I was 6–1, a performance good enough to dispel the gloom of my first demotion only two months before. And from that time on things began to get better, if only slowly. My Japanese was improving, I was able to eat more and more different kinds of food, and my maku-shita rank gave me some status among my stablemates. I was no longer a raw apprentice. During the next two years, though my rise up the sumo pyramid was temporarily stalled at the maku-shita level, I began to get used to heya life and my adopted country. I even took up some Japanese games like *go* to fill my increasing spare time. I've gotten fairly good at *go* over the years. Everyone at the heya is always praising my ability—but I sometimes wonder why they make sure to keep advising me on the moves as they stand around watching and complimenting.

Another heartening thing as I entered my second year was that I was gaining weight at last. From the incredible low of 205 pounds in January I was back up around 250 pounds by the following May, just in time to flunk my draft physical. My one-year exemption from military duty granted by the governor of Hawaii just before I left for Japan had expired. I was called to the U.S. camp at Zama near Tokyo, but I weighed in at some fifteen pounds over the maximum for my height and was sent back to less lethal battles in the sumo ring. I was summoned once again three years later in 1968, when pressing personnel needs for the expanding war in Vietnam led the army to create a special bootcamp for overweights. But my wrestling career was saved again from a premature end as I was declared ineligible, this time because of the injury to my vocal cord.

The ambassador intercedes
It's really ironic. During my first year at the stable I probably would have jumped at any opportunity to go home. But when my first chance came I refused to go. In June of 1966, at a time when I was becoming fully adjusted to the life of a sumotori, the Sumo Association scheduled a good-will exhibition tour to Hawaii including Maui, similar to the tour in 1964 when I had met Takasago and been invited to the heya. Since a number of lower-ranked wrestlers always accompany the sekitori on the jaunts to serve as tsukebito, my friends and supporters in Hawaii were naturally anxious for me to come, and the association complied with their wishes by extending me an invitation just before the May Tokyo basho that year. But I refused, explaining that I had lost three tournaments in a row and needed to stay in Japan and practice. Association officials called me during and after the tournament to see if I wouldn't change my mind, but I continued to say no, giving additional excuses such as that I wanted to be a sekitori for my first return home.

My losing performances, however, had little to do with my reluctance to join the group, and, in fact, I had a winning 5–2 at the May basho just before the Hawaii trip. The real reason was that my boss, Takasago, who as head of the tour division of the Association should have led the group as he had two years earlier, was not going. For during that 1964 trip, which included brief stops in Los Angeles and San Francisco as well as Hawaii, an unfortunate incident took place for which Takasago was held responsible. Several wrestlers bought pistols on the U.S. west coast and brought them, illegally, into Japan. Perhaps most had just wanted them as souvenirs, but the association became embroiled in scandal when one wrestler sold a few of his purchases to a gangster. In the ensuing commotion Takasago was disqualified from the 1966 trip. Although I was unable to explain why to the association and the people back in Hawaii,. it was my feeling of loyalty to the man who had scouted me in Hawaii and given me my chance in sumo that was at the center of my reluctance. Though sumo stables usually have several oyakata, many wrestlers feel a particular father-son bond with the one oyakata who was directly responsible for bringing them into the heya. This is one of the major reasons that some sumotori leave a stable with an oyakata when he breaks away to form a new heya, and there has been at least one case where a high-ranking wrestler threatened to quit the sport if he was not permitted to leave with the man to whom he felt the greatest loyalty. Even though I was the deshi of all the Takasago-beya oyakata, I felt especially that I was Takasago's deshi. On my first return home, I wanted him to take me.

The pressure on me to change my mind was intense. Supporters in Hawaii, like the members of the 442nd Veteran's Club, were shocked to hear that their favorite sumo son was not making the trip and wrote to the association to make sure I was on the plane. Letters poured in from Maui from people like the principal of Baldwin High School. Even the governor of Hawaii himself wrote. And the man appointed to head the group, the stablemaster of Nishonoseki-beya, came to plead with Takasago to make me give in. But I remained adamant. What finally forced me to change my mind was the intercession of American Ambassador Edwin Reischauer. After receiving a letter from the Hawaiian governor, Reischauer called Takasago to make a special appeal. Takasago then told me to make the trip.

My stubborn refusal had assumed the proportions of a minor international incident and made it necessary to mend some fences. On the night before the tour left for Hawaii, I visited Japanese Foreign Minister Etsusaburo Shiina to express my regrets for all the trouble I had caused. And after reaching Hawaii, I had to apologize to almost everyone I met, including the governor. But surprisingly, the affair did little to mar the warm reception I received everywhere we went in Hawaii. It was terrific, especially on Maui, with huge crowds turning out to greet me. I was really surprised at how popular I was.

When I saw some of the sekitori try surfing, I was reminded again of what great balance the best wrestlers have and that the key to achieving it is strong legs and hips. Taiho, Kitanofuji, Tamanoumi, all picked it up in no time and became quite skilled, despite their massive weight.

During the three days we spent on Maui, I was reunited briefly with my family and old friends, who were all anxious to see me work out. The second day of exhibition bouts happened to fall on my twenty-second birthday, and my mother was in the front row of spectators. Seizing an opportunity for some fun, several of the top-ranked wrestlers decided to give me a little birthday razzing in front of the hometown fans. They got me in the ring and put me through some butsukari-geiko, roughing it up a little by shoving me around the ring or pushing me over every time I tried to struggle to my feet. It was nothing much, but a wrestler came up right after to tell me my mother was crying. If she'd only known what I'd been through in the Takasago keikoba.

Takamiyama practices pushing during jungyo. Above right, *two wrestlers battle it out under the sun.* Below right, *sumotori take on the local youngsters—and lose.*

Jungyo *performances are often set out of doors. The crowd gathers around the temporary arena, and children perch in the trees. But it is not a holiday for the young wrestlers* (right and below) *who work right through from four in the morning till nine or ten at night.*

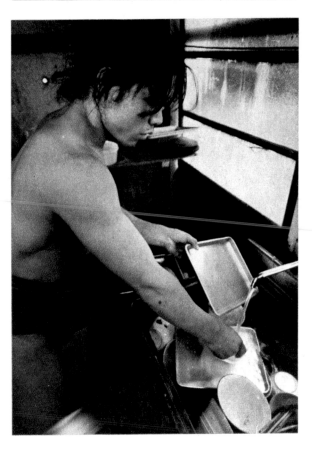

Despite my early reluctance to participate, the Hawaii tour turned out to be a major turning point in my career because it built my confidence tremendously. When people congratulated me, when they shook my hand and said "Jesse, you're doing a wonderful job for Hawaii," it made me proud. I wanted to go back to Japan and buckle down. I think feeling all those people behind me really made the difference, and was a major reason I had winning tournaments for almost two straight years after I got back.

Jungyo

Soon after returning to Japan to continue my assault on the juryo division, I took part in my first extended *jungyo* or exhibition tour, a month-long trip in August 1966 through northern Honshu and Hokkaido. Sumotori stage exhibition bouts throughout the year between official basho, both at home and abroad. Jungyo vary from one-day exhibition tournaments such as that held every year at the annual festival of the Yasukuni shrine in Tokyo which honors Japan's war dead to extended jaunts of a month or more throughout the Japanese countryside. Sometimes unofficial basho are staged, known as *junhonbasho,* in contrast to the six official tournaments, *honbasho*. The results of these unofficial competitions do not count, but there are prizes awarded as at the honbasho. During my first couple of years in sumo there were junhonbasho in Hiroshima in April and in Osaka in October, but they have been discontinued. The only one now is a week-long tournament in Sendai, north of Tokyo, at the end of July after the Nagoya basho. I have won the Sendai junhonbasho twice, and collected two color television sets for my pains— a far cry from those days when my nose was pressed against the drugstore window.

Domestic jungyo serve to promote sumo at the grass-roots level and to give fans who live far from the four cities where the major tournaments take place a chance to see their favorites in person. Overseas jungyo introduce Japan's national sport to a wider audience. But with the constant traveling and fighting over and above the six regular basho, the sumotori's life is a busy and exhausting one with very little free time.

Overseas jungyo have been popular since Yokozuna Hitachiyama and three other wrestlers made a goodwill trip to the United States and several European countries in late 1907 and early 1908. In Washington, the group met President Theodore Roosevelt and demonstrated fighting techniques and ceremonies. A cartoon from the time, which pointed out the many weighty problems the American president faced, shows Roosevelt struggling to lift the huge, pot-bellied Hitachiyama. On the wrestler's body are written "Congress," "Panama Canal," "Railroads," "Financial Depression," "Trusts," "Fleet to the Pacific," and "Third Term." With the Hitachiyama trip providing the spark, tours were soon dispatched to London, Taiwan, Korea, Manchuria, and the Siberian city of Vladivostok.

More recently, grand champions Taiho and Kashiwado led a group of wrestlers

on an epoch-making trip to Russia in the summer of 1965 which included an
exhibition tournament in Moscow. A tour of China will have taken place by April
1973, to help commemorate the normalization of relations with Japan. Most
numerous have been the jungyo to Hawaii where a large population of Japanese
ancestry not only avidly follows the professional sport but also organizes local
amateur sumo groups such as the one on Maui where I got my start. It was
while he was on a jungyo that I first met Takasago. There are now regular jungyo to Hawaii every other year. I like to think that my own rise in sumo has
helped to spread its popularity to groups outside Japan, both in Hawaii and elsewhere.

For the young wrestlers who accompany the sekitori on tour as tsukebito, a
long jungyo is, if possible, even more exhausting than life in the heya in Tokyo.
My first jungyo was in April 1965, when I served under the juryo sekitori Hibikiya during the Hiroshima junhonbasho. But since the trip was a short one
confined to a single city, it was not until the August jungyo the following year
that I had my first taste of life on the road. I was assigned as one of three tsukebito to maegashira Fujinishiki. We traveled by train for over a month all the
way to Hokkaido and back, visiting a different town every day where we
practiced and staged bouts in temporary rings set up by local people. Since
there are no official tournaments staged north of Tokyo, I was excited at having
my first chance to see the North country, but with all the work I had to do I
hardly had time to see a thing. Let me describe a typical day on that jungyo to
give an idea what these tours are like.

Jungyo exhibitions are sometimes held inside local halls or stadiums, but most
of the time that summer we were outside. I had to get up at four every morning
to hurry to the exhibition ground to compete with the tsukebito of other wrestlers
for a good place to set up a makeshift dressing room for Fujinishiki. The area
was enclosed by a large canvas to regulate admission. The canvas was put up
by the yobidashi and the drivers of the two association trucks which accompany
the tour to carry the heavy equipment. Since there was only a limited amount
of space along one side of the canvas that was suitable for dressing rooms, the
tsukebito who came late had to set up outside the canvas. They caught hell from
their sekitori who prefered to be within the more private confines of the canvas,
away from the crowds milling about outside. After staking my claim, I had to
help haul the gear from the trucks: the tent, the pots, pans, and charcoal stoves
used to prepare the morning meal; and the *akeni*, the foot lockers that accompany each sekitori wrestler on tour and contain his mawashi, *kesho-mawashi*
(the richly embroidered aprons worn for the entering-the-ring ceremony), and
other accoutrements that don't go into his personal luggage.

Setting up the tent and the cooking area took until about six when I put on
my mawashi and began a two-hour workout with the other tsukebito. For even
on jungyo there was no let-up in practive. We usually trained on the flat ground
instead of on the one dohyo reserved for the bouts later on. Because the ground

is hard, your feet get painfully sore, and falling down, though inevitable, left you bruised and aching. The sekitori arrived between seven-thirty and eight to go through their workouts. When they finished, they were taken to a local bathhouse to be washed by some of the senior tsukebito while the younger boys stayed back to cook the meal.

The exhibition began around ten each morning with bouts between the lowest-ranking members of the jungyo and ended around three in the afternoon with matches between the ozeki and yokozuna. The younger guys had to keep one eye on the dohyo as they served the food to make sure they didn't miss their bout. I fought a bit later since I was already fairly high up the maku-shita division. On rainy days the exhibitions were cancelled if less than two hundred people had assembled to watch. If more turned out, we went ahead with a shortened version of the regular show called *sakuradori*. In sakuradori, the usual order is reversed with the yokozuna wrestling first to give the people a chance to see at least the most popular sekitori. On such days the lower-ranking sumotori are excused.

After serving the meal and quickly wolffing down what was left, I helped wash the cooking utensils and pack them back into boxes before loading them on the trucks. I was also constantly taking wet towels or cold drinks to Fuji-nishiki and the other perspiring sekitori who were relaxing playing cards or mahjong. And time would have to be found at some point to dash off to the bathhouse, which was often a good distance from the exhibition ground, without missing my turn in the ring. Just before the entering-the-ring ceremony preceding the upper division bouts, I took Fujinishiki's heavy kesho-mawashi out of his akeni and helped him into it. When he returned I got him out of the apron and into his regular mawashi for his match. Then, as the day's program neared the end, the tents had to be taken down and carried with the rest of the gear to the trucks.

When the exhibition was over, the sekitori left by bus or taxi for the railroad station. The tsukebito had to walk, carrying their luggage and our own. If the station was far away, we tried to hitch a ride. The special sumo train left around four and, depending on the distance, reached the town holding the next day's exhibition two to five hours later. It was slow because, being unscheduled, we kept having to wait for other trains to pass. The train had eight coaches, two first-class and six second-class. The first-class coaches were reserved for the oyakata on the tour, the highest-ranking referees, and the maku-uchi wrestlers. There were numerically enough seats for everyone, but one train seat is a pretty cramped space for a sumotori so a lot of the guys would pull rank and take two apiece, forcing the lowliest onto the floor.

When we reached our destination around seven or eight the entourage separated into groups to go to the various *ryokan* (inns), the sekitori and oyakata by car, me and the rest on foot. We usually were assigned to inns by stable, but sometimes over one third of the 350-man tour was put in a single hotel in areas like hot-spring resorts which had extensive facilities. If there were no inns, we stayed in private homes. After arriving at the inn I had to go from room to room bowing and giving formal greetings to the sekitori. Then I helped bathe Fujinishiki before serving the evening meal, brought by the people at the ryokan. The sekitori usually retire as soon as possible and the tsukebito, like all good nannies, must make sure he has the things he needs such as his toothbrush and pyjamas. When Fujinishiki was finally bedded down for the night, I had my own dinner, washed out some clothes, and headed for the bath, all the while vowing to reach the juryo division fast as the contented snores of the sekitori filled the building. It was close to midnight before I collapsed on to the futon— after setting the alarm for 4:00 A.M., when the whole thing would begin again.

That jungyo was agony. I got little sleep and, although I was in maku-shita myself, I was constantly being razzed by more senior maku-shita wrestlers with greater tour experience. I realize now that they were doing it partly because it was my first tour and I had a lot to learn, but there were times when I really wanted to wreck some guys. My temper got pretty short because I was always exhausted. A different town every day, and every day wrestling, training and chores. Everything I did I dragged. I was so beat I fell asleep the minute I got on the train, even if I was on the floor. There was only one way to avoid going through it all again and to make my next jungyo a more enjoyable one—to become a sekitori.

Takamiyama crouches to receive ken-sho *after a victorious bout.*

VI

New Sekitori

Toward the top: juryo and maku-uchi
With my visit to Hawaii and the summer jungyo providing the great incentives, I added three more 5-2 tournaments to my 5-2 in May of 1966 and rose to maku-shita number two for the 1967 Tokyo New Year's basho. If I could maintain the pace, promotion to juryo was assured. The pressure was on and I gave everything I had in training during December and early January, but after my first two matches my record was only even. Then came the third bout, one of the most exciting moments in my career. For I was to take on a sekitori in a tournament for the first time. To complete pairings and to test how juryo candidates will fare against stiffer competition, men at the top of maku-shita are often put against wrestlers at the bottom of juryo for one or two of their seven fights during a basho. This means that they fight in the juryo division on those days, and have their hair dressed in the fancy *oicho-mage* style reserved for sekitori wrestlers. The *oicho-mage*, a style common in the Tokugawa period, is named after the ginkgo leaf which it is said to resemble. It is far more elaborate than the simple chon-mage which lower-division wrestlers wear—as do sekitori when they are not in the tournament ring or at some formal gathering.

I was really keyed-up to be fighting in juryo and to have my first oicho-mage. All the newspaper reporters came into the dressing room to take my picture and I began to imagine myself already a sekitori. I could almost taste it. I knew I had to make it. There was no way I was going to lose that day. And I didn't. I remember beating him yori-taoshi. Later in the tournament I defeated another juryo wrestler on my way to my fifth consecutive 5-2 performance.

Takasago didn't make me suffer through the usual waiting period before the new banzuke is officially announced. Three days after the basho the judges got together to decide the new rankings while I waited on tenderhooks at the stable. The boss came back. He smiled. I knew I'd made it. To say that I was elated would be putting it mildly indeed. It was the happiest, most exciting moment of my life, even better than when I moved from juryo into the top division later on. The only thing that can possibly compare was my championship in 1972. The feeling was out of this world. This was what I had slaved for for three long years, and it suddenly made all the pain, all the razzing I had taken seem worth it. At last I became a full-fledged wrestler with the right to receive a salary and have people serving under me, to be addressed respectfully as "sekitori" or

"Takamiyama-zeki." Training would of course still be rough if I wanted to maintain my rank and go higher, but I would not have to run around after anyone anymore.

I soon got busy making the rounds of friends and supporters who had backed me up, as all wrestlers must do at important moments or when they receive something. You must give formal greetings, and I remember repeating *"Gottsuan desu,"* the all-purpose phrase used by sumotori to express thanks and joy or when requesting favors, over and over again. A new sekitori needs a large amount of money very quickly to acquire the necessary trappings of his new status, and the benevolence of a patron is vital. Among the things needed were a *montsuki,* the dress kimono worn at formal occasions, and a kesho-mawashi, a heavy, ankle-length apron made of brocaded silk and hemmed with gold fringe that is worn for the colorful entering-the-ring ceremony performed respectively by juryo and maku-uchi wrestlers before the start of their bouts. The custom of wearing such aprons dates back at least as far as the eighteenth century. A single kesho-mawashi can cost up to one thousand dollars and a few of the more elaborate ones cost a great deal more. Some new sekitori have difficulty attracting individual patrons soon enough to have their kesho-mawashi ready for their first basho in juryo, but they are usually helped out by the koenkai of their stable. I was fortunate to receive two right away. One came from Pan Am through the good offices of David Jones. The other was sent by the 442nd Veteran's Club in Hawaii who were told of my promotion in a letter from Mrs. Takasago. I was also the recipient of cash gifts from Hawaii and a montsuki from the president of one of the Takasago-beya koenkai. At the bottom of the kesho-mawashi sent by the 442nd was embroidered the slogan of the old World War Two regiment: "Go For Broke." And that was exactly what I very soon had to do to keep my hard-won rank.

As I went into training for my first tournament in juryo, the Osaka basho of March 1967, bad news came from the Sumo Association. It was decided to cut the number of wrestlers in both the maku-uchi and juryo divisions after the tournament. At that time there were eighteen ranks in juryo with two wrestlers at each one. The reform reduced the number to the present thirteen which meant that far fewer men would be allowed to compete in the division after the May tournament. Having just entered juryo, I was at the bottom at number eighteen. Under normal circumstances I would have to win only a minimum of eight bouts to ensure promotion or at least maintenance of the status quo. But I was told I would have to win at least ten to remain at the lowest number thirteen rung of the revamped juryo ladder.

To make matters worse I suffered a dislocated shoulder during training. It was right after Chiyonoyama broke away from Dewanoumi-beya to found the Kokonoe stable and join the Takasago ichimon. Chiyonoyama took the ozeki Kitanofuji with him into his new stable, and the future yokozuna soon began working out with us in Osaka. I was thrown into the dirt one day by

Kitanofuji, landed badly, and twisted my shoulder. The injury and the pressure to win at least ten bouts made that tournament one of my roughest. It was really like having to make sekitori all over again. Luckily, my shoulder healed sufficiently before the opening day and, though struggling, I was able to record the bare minimum, 10-5, in my first outing in juryo. I just squeaked by. There were guys in juryo with 9-6 records, which usually means a healthy promotion, who fell back down to maku-shita because of the cut. It was quite a relief, but I was still at the very bottom of the division at number thirteen for the May basho.

I really relished those first few months as a sekitori. For the March tournament I was given my first two tsukebito. One was a maku-shita ani-deshi, the other a young guy in jo-nidan. It was a bit strange to begin with, having people serve me, but I guess it's something that's not that hard to get used to. Although my older tsukebito washed and dressed me, I didn't make too many demands on him. In sumo you respect a man who is older than you, even if he is of lower rank and assigned as your servant. Besides I learned a lot from my ani-deshi tsuke-bito who had been around a lot longer than I had and knew a great deal about what a sekitori should wear and how he should act. It was my younger assistant that I made run errands and razzed, in the time-honored tradition that I had learned so well during my years on the other side of the fence.

It was also a great feeling to receive a paycheck, like a guy with his first job, as well as to be occasionally wined and dined by friends and those kind enough to help me out as patrons. There was, too, the excitement of my first jungyo as a sekitori. After the Osaka basho in April of '67 we traveled through a few prefectures along the Japan Sea coast of western Honshu. As a foreigner, I had been in the public eye since breaking into sumo, but my elevation to sekitori seemed to greatly enhance my popularity. It was terrific. Everywhere we went on the tour people wanted to meet me, get my autograph, or offer words of en-couragement. It was pretty heady stuff for a twenty-two-year-old, and I had a hard time believing that I was actually one of the more famous wrestlers in the game. I recalled with a slight shudder all the work and running around I had done on a similar tour less than a year ago. The difference was total. I vowed then and there never to lose my rank.

Fortunately I never did. In fact my new status seemed to suit me so well I started going up pretty fast. I never had a losing performance in juryo, and after five tournaments in the division I was promoted to maku-uchi for the New Year's Basho of 1968. It was a great thrill to make it into the top division, if not quite as exhilarating as my promotion to juryo the year before. My maku-uchi debut was a good one. I was 9-6 as a maegashira number nine and won the fighting spirit award, one of the three special awards given at each tourna-ment, the other two being for technique and outstanding performance. The newspapers had a field day analyzing the new page of sumo history that was being written by the first foreigner to reach the highest division, as they had before when I made sekitori and would again when I won the Emperor's Cup.

I guess I was the first "authentic" foreigner to do all these heroic things. There have been citizens of other nations who have become sekitori and entered maku-uchi, most notably a number of Koreans and one American. But the Koreans were and are largely men born and raised in Japan whose nationality alone distinguishes them from Japanese wrestlers. And the American, Kiichiro Ozaki, who reached the top division in 1944 under the name of Toyonishiki, was the son of Japanese parents and presumably had no trouble passing for Japanese during the war. I know personally of only one other true gaijin who has tried the sport, an American from California who joined Hanakago-beya in 1968. He was a good prospect, winning a championship in jo-nidan and working his way up to the middle of sandanme. I never knew him very well and don't know why he left. I remember meeting him one night and he kept calling me Jesse in front of other wrestlers. I don't mind any friends calling me Jesse, but in the sumo world a lower-ranked wrestler just doesn't refer to a sekitori by his given name. He must use "sekitori" or add either "san" of "zeki" to the wrestling name. I was quite embarrassed in front of the other wrestlers who told me to give him a good talk on sumo etiquette. Believe me, I know how hard it is for someone from a completely different cultural background to make it in sumo society, but if you want to be a sumotori you just have to accept the life-style that goes with it.

Gishiki, television, bright lights, and saké

The kesho-mawashi I wore for my first entering-the-ring ceremony in juryo was certainly the most dazzling symbol of my new sekitori status. And as I paraded in and out of the ring with the other members of the division, I was suddenly conscious of being a very small part of a long ceremonial tradition which epito-mizes the dignity and formality of sumo and sets it apart from most other spectator sports. The entering-the-ring ceremony *(dohyo-iri)* is only one of several *gishiki* (ceremonies, rituals) performed by various actors and comprising the ancient pageantry which takes place every day of the basho and serves to orna-ment, glorify and consecrate the bouts themselves.

But to offset the solemnity of the gishiki there are the saké-swilling, picnicking fans, crammed four to a tiny box, yelling the names of their favorite gladiators and adding just the right touch of iconoclasm. And over the whole scene, which was once dedicated to the gods, hover the lights and cameras of the new deity, tele-vision, recording and in some cases dictating what goes on below. The whole potpourri somehow manages to come together to create that total and unique environment known as a sumo basho. Though watching the medium in your own living room is the next best thing, the only real way to get the message is to make a trip to the Kokugikan in Tokyo or to one of the other tournament cities.

The drama starts early in the morning the day before the tournament opens. Yobidashi parade through the streets in two teams beating the *taiko,* a large drum suspended from a long pole and carried by two bearers, to announce that a honbasho is about to take place. Inside the arena, at ten o'clock in the morning, the *dohyo-matsuri* (blessing-the-ring ritual) begins, an ancient shinto rite that perpetuates the tradition of shinji-zumo. The dohyo-matsuri is meant to purify the battleground for the coming fifteen days of action, to make sure that no accidents occur, and to signify the wrestlers' pledge that they will fight in a correct and dignified fashion. The prayers offered to the various gods of heaven and earth also appeal for good weather (a holdover from earlier times when bouts were staged outside), good crops, and protection from calamity and disaster. Officiating are three *gyoji*, members of a profession whose men serve as sumo high priests and also referee the bouts themselves. Around the dohyo sit the oyakata who serve as judges during the tournament.

Two wooden sticks are clapped together—like those used in kabuki plays— and the gyoji begin reciting the first of many invocations in the sing-song, man- nered style of an earlier era. In the course of the ceremony, short wooden stakes decorated with jagged paper strips similar to those hanging from the yokozuna's belt are placed at the four corners. Saké is sprinkled in the four corners, the four directions, and in the center of the ring. Further offerings are made, and saké is served to the assembled judges. As the ritual ends, the two groups of taiko- beating yobidashi file into the arena and march repeatedly around the ring— before marching out to perform a similar routine at each stable. A briefer dohyo- matsuri is also held at each heya to bless the practice dohyo on the day preceding the start of practice for each tournament.

The action begins the following day. In Tokyo it takes place in the Kokugikan, a large hall capable of seating ten thousand. At the center is the dohyo, the clay, sand-surfaced mound into which are sunk straw, earth-filled bales along the four sides of the square and in the center to delineate the circle where the fights take place. In the middle of the ring are inlaid two white lines where sumotori toe the mark during their warming-up rituals and where they crouch for the tachi- ai. Suspended over the battleground, as a reminder of the days when spectators were not protected from the elements, is a wooden roof in an ancient religious architectural style called *shinmei-zukuri*, often seen at sacred Japanese sites such as the grand shrines at Ise. Hanging down from the roof at the four corners are huge tassels (*fusa*) of green, red, white, and black. The tassels are said to sym- bolize elements in a complex Chinese philosophical system concerning the origins of the universe. They represent the gods of the four directions and the four sea- sons: *seiryu*, green, god of the east—spring; *shujyaku*, red, god of the south— summer; *hakko*, white, god of the west—autumn; and *genbu*, black, god of the north—winter. From the tassels sprout the ubiquitous strips of white, zig-zag paper. Until 1952, there were pillars at the four corners with bunting of the ap- propriate color draped around them, but they were removed in favor of the tassels to allow the spectators a less restricted view of the action. But the fans complaints, voiced vehemently long before 1952, were only part of the reason. It is hardly a coincidence that television broadcasts of sumo tournaments began in 1953.

Radiating outward from the center to the rear of the hall are a series of ground-floor boxes (*masu* or *sajiki*), tiny cubicles separated from each other by low wooden railings in which four people are meant to squat on cushions (*zabuton*). Although the general public can usually secure a box in the rear, the best masu close to the ring are held by the *chaya* (literally, teahouses), a limited number of booths, lined colorfully along both sides of the entrance to the Kokugikan, whose employees guide their customers to their seats and bring them food and drink. The chaya divide the best seats among favored clients such as businesses and government departments on a tournament or season basis. There have been outcries of elitism by those unable to obtain good masu, and in 1957 an official of the Sumo Association tried unsuccessfully to commit suicide when the issue was brought before the Diet. There have been reforms, but it is still necessary to get an invitation from a friend in an organization holding a well-located masu to get near the action.

Two other kinds of seats are the *suna-kaburi* and balcony chairs. The suna-kaburi (sand-covered) are the best seats in the house because they are closest to the ring in front of the first rows of masu. They get their name from the fact that spectators sitting on cushions so close to the ring are often sprayed with sand when the action just above gets fast and furious. And there is always the danger of finding yourself with over six hundred pounds of beef in your lap if the two combatants topple violently off the dohyo. No refreshments are served there and the choice positions are usually held over the years by distinguished patrons or lovers of the sport. The balcony resembles theaters in the West and, although far from the ring, often provides a better view than the masu at the very back of the ground floor. Balcony chairs are also recommended for those who find it painful to sit cross-legged for hours at a stretch. High in the rafters above the balcony along each wall hang the huge commemorative pictures of tournament winners from the recent past. If you get out your field glasses and study the faces, you'll see that one of them looks suspiciously like me.

For the fan in the masu, sumo is really one big picnic. Squeezed together in their tiny cubicles, tight against their neighbors, the spectators gaily feast on a mountain of food and drink brought in baskets by attendants dressed in old-fashioned pantaloons and kimono. Roast chicken on sticks, rice, dried squid, fruit, peanuts and potato chips are only a few of the delicacies that are to be washed down with saké, beer, soft drinks and tea. If you haven't gone on an empty stomach, you are allowed to take home the leftovers in a bag kindly provided for the purpose. In the constant bustle some fans probably miss a lot of the action, but on the other hand they create an awful lot of their own, especially after the first few cups of saké. For they are as important in the drama of a sumo basho as the wrestlers themselves.

The hall fills up sometime after three as the crowd streams in to catch the bouts of the sekitori wrestlers in juryo and maku-uchi. (Television broadcasts begin at four and concentrate only on maku-uchi matches.) But to get an idea of how high the pyramid of sumotori on which the sekitori stand really is, you should get there by about 10:30 or 11:00 in the morning when the show begins with the raw apprentices in maezumo. If you do, you will be treated to one of the best bargains I know of in the sports world, over one hundred and fifty sumo bouts which last until six in the evening when the yokozuna finally ascend the dohyo. Besides, you can have any seat in the house until the hall begins to fill in the afternoon. Bouts are staged in ascending order of rank, with the crescendo of excitement gradually building throughout the day as better and better wrestlers successively go through their paces until the peak is reached in late afternoon when the highest-ranking men take the stage. The higher a wrestler's rank, the more time he is allowed to go through the warming-up exercises and rituals and the greater the amount of props he is permitted to use. The young lads in mae-zumo merely ascend the ring, bow, clap their hands and charge. The sekitori in juryo and maku-uchi go through a three- or four-minute series of preliminaries which purify the mind, cleanse the body and build up the tension—for them and the crowd.

At about three—the schedule is pushed up roughly thirty minutes on the final day of each basho to allow television to cover a part of the awards ceremony at the end—the real spectacle begins as the juryo division files in to perform their dohyo-iri, a ceremony which is repeated later by the maku-uchi wrestlers before the commencement of bouts in their division. The dohyo-iri is staged consecutively in two groups with one entering from the east, the other from the west, a holdover from the days of team competition. Led by a gyoji, the sumotori file down the *hanamichi* (flower path), often fighting their way through the milling throngs. Dressed in their kesho-mawashi, they are ceremonially introduced, individually, as they ascend the dohyo and parade around the circle. When the last man is up they turn to the center, clap their hands, raise their right arms, lift their aprons slightly with the left hand, raise both arms, then turn and file out the way the came. The ritual is short but colorful and to first-time observers, quite humorous. The dohyo-iri gives the audience a chance to be introduced to and compare the wrestlers. And, like all sumo gishiki, it carries meaning. The hand-clapping shows that the body has been purified. Raising the arms and the kesho-mawashi is said to symbolize the shiko exercise done in training and before the bout itself. These actions could also demonstrate that the sumotori is carrying no concealed weapons.

A special version of the dohyo-iri is performed on the one day a year when the emperor comes to view the action from his special second-floor box. The wrestlers file in from east and west as usual, but instead of forming a circle on the dohyo, they line up in rows facing the imperial box and simultaneously raise their legs and stamp the ground (*soroi-bumi*). Then they squat down and rise individually to bow as they are introduced. Times have changed with Japan's democratization; wrestlers once went to the emperor, today he comes to them.

After the maku-uchi dohyo-iri, the yokozuna enter individually to go through the moving yokozuna dohyo-iri (yokozuna ring-entering ceremony). The grand champion is accompanied by his *tachi-mochi* (sword-bearer) and his *tsuyu-harai* (literally dew-remover, a herald or forerunner), and all three men wear matching kesho-mawashi, a luxurious set of aprons that runs the yokozuna into considerable expense. In the past the tachi-mochi made sure the unarmed yokozuna had a sword at the ready should any samurai spectator get unruly; the tsuyu-harai cleared a path for him to tread. Today, the two men are maku-uchi division wrestlers, usually stablemates of the grand champion.

The gyoji enters the ring first and squats down. Then the yokozuna, wearing the massive white belt that indicates his rank, climbs up with his two attendants who remain squatting throughout the ceremony. The grand champion's solemn, studied movements convey the solemnity, power, and grandeur of the man most responsible for exemplifying the dignity of the sport. Squatting flanked by his attendants, he first swings his arms over his head in a full circle before bringing his hands together with a great clap to attract the attention of the gods. After rubbing his palms together he repeats the motion, but this time finishes by extending his arms to the side and opening his hands to show they are empty. He then rises and goes to the center of the ring. There he repeats the hand-clapping and palm-opening, but this time follows these gestures with three mighty shiko to scare away any persistent demons not cleansed at the dohyo-matsuri before the basho opened. After stomping each foot, he bends fully at the knees with one hand on his chest, the other extended, and his eyes fixed straight ahead, then moves his feet slowly together by wriggling his feet in the dirt until he is upright. Each stamp of the foot brings a roar from the crowd. When he has finished at stage center, he returns to squat between his attendants and repeat the same motions he performed at the outset. Finally he rises, bows, and files out with his attendents, the gyoji bringing up the rear. The entire yokozuna dohyo-iri is said to represent a prayer to the gods for tranquility in the universe and peace and abundance in the nation.

After the dohyo-iri the maku-uchi wrestlers return to the shitaku-beya one of two enormous dressing rooms at the back of the building. Here they change out of their kesho-mawashi and into their tournament mawashi to await their bouts. The shitaku-beya used throughout the day by all divisions, is a long, open-plan room with a wide raised platform around three sides. At one end, nearest the entrance, is a bath. The wrestlers and their tsukebito sit on straw mats along the raised sections. The end farthest from the bath is reserved for the yokozuna and some six or seven wrestlers serving him. Along the two sides are the other maku-uchi sumotori and their assistants, with the ozeki located closest to the yokozuna, the sekiwake next to them, and so on down to the lowest men in the division nearest the bath. Just before a wrestler leaves the shitaku-beya, one of his tsukebito will carry the personal cushion with his name on it (*basho-buton*) out to the arena to be placed beside the ring where the wrestler will wait to fight, bringing back the cushion of the wrestler who is already in the ring.

Around 4:30, after a short intermission to sweep the dohyo and change the judges, the bouts in the maku-uchi division begin. Each wrestler enters the arena while the combatants in the second bout before his own are going through their preliminaries. He sits down on his cushion below the dohyo roughly at the same time as his opponent, who enters from the other dressing room and is seated across the ring. When it's time, the yobidashi (name-caller) climbs into the ring to face, in turn, the east and west, extend his fan, and warble the name of each combatant in a high-pitched, stylized voice. The referee then announces them again as the two wrestlers ascend the dohyo to begin a series of pre-liminary rituals which include shiko, presumably to frighten away any personal demons, salt throwing, purification of mind and body with water, and *shikiri*—toeing the mark when the wrestlers crouch facing each other at the starting lines with fists in the dirt. Each of these actions is repeated several times.

Salt throwing is meant to purify the battleground and is a privilege allowed only to those wrestlers in maku-shita and above. The symbolic cleansing with water is permitted only for sekitori in juryo and maku-uchi. This cleansing is one of the first acts performed after entering the ring. The wrestler is offered a ladle of water (*chikara-mizu* or "power water") from a bucket in one corner by either the winner of the previous bout from the same side of the dohyo or from the wrestler waiting to fight from the same direction if the previous man has lost; for a loser would be unable to offer strength and might jinx the next man. Chikara-mizu also signifies that the wrestlers will fight with full strength. The wrestler rinses his mouth with the chikara-mizu and spits behind *chikara-gami*, "power paper," a piece of tissue paper which he has received from the same donor. With the mind purified, the sumotori uses the chikara-gami to symbolically cleanse his body by wiping his armpits. Chikara-gami is also said to carry the symbolic meaning of crushing any wickedness hiding under the feet.

These preliminaries, which I will come back to when I describe in detail one of my own bouts, are often a boringly repetitious postponement of the moment of truth for the uninitiated spectator, and they last longer than the action itself. But for the sumo aficionado who can often tell a great deal about a wrestler's mental preparation or the way he may be planning his attack by watching the way he goes through each motion, this posturing is an important element in his total enjoyment. And, of course, for the two men in the ring the psy-chological warfare which characterizes the shikiri is an essential part of the struggle. Those who fail to get drawn into this prefight drama may watch the other spectators or take comfort in the fact that there used to be no time limit at all. The combatants were permitted to wait until just the proper psychological peak had been reached, no matter how long it took. In 1928 a ten-minute time limit was enforced in the maku-uchi division which was then gradually reduced. But the gods who control television's tight scheduling were still not satisfied, so the limit was reduced again. Today maku-uchi sumotori are given four minutes to get themselves "up," men in juryo three, those in maku-shita two, and those in the lower divisions even less.

Another short intermission follows the completion of the first half of the maku-uchi bouts, during which time the judges are changed again and the chief gyoji announces the next day's pairings by holding up pieces of paper bearing the names of the opponents and calling them out. The beautifully lettered characters are written by the gyoji themselves. In the second half comes the climax of the day with bouts featuring wrestlers in the three sanyaku ranks and the yokozuna.

The long, exciting day comes to a close with the spectacular *yumitori-shiki* or bow ceremony. This ceremony originated in 1575 when one of Japan's greatest military leaders, Oda Nobunaga, presented one of his favorite bows to Miai Ganzaemon, the winner of a grand tournament held in his presence. The victor was so delighted with the honor that he danced twirling the bow as a gesture of thanks. Winning sanyaku sumotori were once presented with gifts after their bouts on the last day of the tournament (*senshuraku*). Komusubi received an arrow, sekiwake a bowstring, and ozeki a bow. The ozeki would then perform the bow ceremony to formally close the tournament and express the joy of all the victorious wrestlers. Even today, sanyaku wrestlers who win on the final day receive symbolic arrows with their prize money as they leave the ring.

The yumitori-shiki is now performed every day to give more people a chance to see it, but not by an ozeki. A special bow twirler is selected from the ranks of wrestlers, usually at the maku-shita level, who makes the ritual his speciality. Dressed in a luxurious kesho-mawashi, he twirls the bow over his head, passes it behind his back, scoops the dirt with it, and finally rests it on his shoulders to perform the shiko and slow rise from a crouch not unlike a part of the yokozuna dohyo-iri.

The main actors in the tournament drama, besides the sumotori themselves, are the gyoji, *shimpan* (judges), and yobidashi. Certainly the most flashy is the gyoji dressed in ancient ceremonial court robes (*hitatare*) of gorgeous colors and patterns and crowned with the black gauze headgear (*eboshi*) of the court nobleman. The gyoji officiates at all sumo ceremonies such as the dohyo-matsuri and dohyo-iri, but his most important job is that of referee. Wielding his *gunbai* or war fan, the gyoji is responsible for supervising every aspect of the bout from the time the wrestlers climb on to the dohyo until they leave. He extends the gunbai and calls out their names as they come up; stands over them with raised gunbai to make sure they perform the shikiri correctly; and informs them formally that the preliminaries are over and the bouts must begin, both verbally and by crouching down facing them and bending the gunbai over backwards with a flick of the wrist. He shouts constant encouragement when the combatants are locked together (*hakkiyoi*, roughly "keep it moving") or when the movement around the ring is furious (*nokotta*, "you're still in the ring"); stops the action in case of injury; freezes the fighters in place with a whack on the back of the belt to tighten a mawashi that has come loose; separates the wrestlers for a brief rest (mizu-iri) if they become exhausted during a long bout, then carefully puts them back in the identical positions to continue; determines the victor with a quick point of the gunbai to the east or west; and, when prize money has been offered by a sponsor, places the envelope on the gunbai and extends it to the victor.

The gyoji is not, however, the ultimate authority. Although he is required to point the gunbai in the winner's direction immediately after the bout, his decision can be overruled by the oyakata judges seated around the ring. In this sense the gyoji can become a pitiable, helpless figure, despite the majesty of his dress and actions. With only his naked eye to determine whether a knee or elbow touched out first before two sumotori crash simultaneously off the dohyo, he must, in the proverbial words of the baseball umpire, call it the way he sees it. But unlike the men in blue, his decision may not be final.

Any one of the shimpan can raise his hand after a close match and call for a mono-ii, a judges' conference in the ring center. During the powwow, the head judge is permitted to make use of an earphone to hear from a judge in a room outside the main hall what the bout looked like in slow-motion videotape replay. During the conference the gyoji may be consulted, but he has no vote in the final decision. The judges, after weighing both human and electronic evidence, can uphold the referee, order a rematch (tori-naoshi), or overturn the original decision (sashi-chigae, changing the direction of the gunbai).

Although it rarely if ever happens, it states in the sumo book of rules that a wrestler waiting below the dohyo to fight may also call for a mono-ii. Should this happen, the wrestler is not included in the judges' conference and thus has no vote. Wrestlers involved in a bout that results in a mono-ii wait in separate corners off the dohyo, praying.

While a tori-naoshi is not held against the gyoji, a sashi-chigae is, and too many of these black marks can lead to demotion or, in extreme cases, premature retirement. The tate-gyoji (chief referee) wears a symbolic sword and it is said that one of its purposes in the past was for committing hara-kiri should he be judged wrong.

The ultimate powerlessness of the gyoji does not stem from any lack of experience or professional competence. Far from it. The recruit devotes his life to the job. Like the sumotori, he begins his career as a young teenager and faces a long climb up the rank structure at the end of a five-year training period. Becoming a tate-gyoji is perhaps even more difficult than achieving the rank of yokozuna, since older referees do not have to retire until they reach sixty-five and there is a strict seniority system. The referees have their own stable (gyoji-beya), headed by the tate-gyoji. There are about thirty gyoji in all although regulations permit up to forty-five and each is named either Kimura or Shikimori in the tradition of two gyoji houses from the pre-Tokugawa warrior days. There were no gyoji during the period of sechie-zumo. The era of buke-zumo produced the first ancestors of the present-day referee and there were gyoji families in various parts of the country. The Kimura and Shikimori houses remained in the Tokugawa period when sumo became fully organized, and the practice of using these two names has been kept even though modern gyoji are not literal descendants.

A gyoji's rank may be seen by looking at his feet and the long, tasseled string which hangs from his gunbai. Low-ranked referees are barefooted. Those officiating at bouts involving wrestlers below the top two rungs of maku-shita ornament the gunbai with black, blue, or green. Gyoji refereeing in juryo and above wear white *tabi* (traditional Japanese socks), and the tassled strings are green and white for juryo bouts, pink and white for those between maegashira, and scarlet for contests involving the sanyaku ranks. The gyoji for sanyaku bouts and the tate-gyoji above him are permitted to wear straw sandals over their tabi. At the top of the rank pyramid stand the two tate-gyoji, although both posts are not always filled. Just below the summit is Shikimori Inosuke who controls the two bouts prior to the final one and sports purple and white gunbai decoration. The yokozuna of the gyoji world is Kimura Shonosuke, whose solid purple string shows that he alone is qualified to officiate at the last bout of the day (*musubi-no-ichiban*) when the grand champion makes his appearance. If there is no Shonosuke during a certain period, Inosuke will preside at the last two bouts. When one Shonosuke retires, the incumbent Inosuke is usually promoted to the top, but this is not invariably the case. Similarly, if Inosuke moves up, the gyoji below him might be elevated or the Inosuke post left open until he or someone else is deemed qualified.

Shimpan are appointed for one-year terms from the 105 oyakata of the Sumo Association. They not only judge the bouts, but also make up the match pairings two days in advance and make recommendations for rank promotions which are usually accepted by the association's board of directors. The number of shimpan varies with the rank of the sumotori in the ring. Make-uchi and juryo bouts rate five, maku-shita four, and the lower ranks three or four. One of the judges always serves as timekeeper, raising his right hand to inform the gyoji when the time limit for the preliminary rituals is reached.

Judges sit on all four sides of the dohyo and are changed frequently like the gyoji, although many return to preside a second time in the course of the long day. The head judge sits alone on the north side which is known as the front (*shomen*). The judges at the east (*higashi-damari* or "eastern waiting place") and west (*nishi-damari* or "western waiting place") sit between two wrestlers waiting to fight. The south-side (*muko-jomen* or "other" side across from sho-men) judge sits beside the gyoji who is waiting his turn to referee. When there are five shimpan, two judges are placed on the south.

Videotape replays were not used by shimpan during the mono-ii until May 1969. Sumo bouts are short and the speed and closeness of certain falls make an instant decision almost impossible, as the gyoji is all too well aware. Watching the slow-motion replays on television, viewers could frequently pick up judging errors, but there was no appealing a shimpan verdict. The issue came to a head on the second day of the March tournament in Osaka in 1969. Yokozuna Taiho had won forty-five straight bouts and was gunning for Futabayama's record of sixty-nine in a row. In a close call at the edge, the gyoji awarded the bout to Taiho, but the judges overruled him in the mono-ii and gave the match to his opponent, Toda (later known as Haguroiwa). Taiho's string was broken. But the video replays and pictures on the following day's sports pages showed clearly that Toda's right foot was half in the sand outside the straw circle while Taiho was still completely in bounds. The outcry over this and another clear error in the same basho involving the man who eventually went on to win the Emperor's Cup led the association to allow the use of videotape from the following tournament. Unfortunately for Taiho, the ruling was not made retroactive.

The yobidashi's name is extremely misleading, for calling the fighters to the fray is only a minor part of his heavy duties. He is really the workhorse of the sumo world. Yobidashi not only construct the dohyo itself, but also keep it swept and neat during the day's bouts and clean up afterwards. They offer towels and water to each wrestler just before the tachiai and to the victors who have just finished, place and remove the wrestlers' cushions, carry the advertising banners around the ring before sponsored bouts, and do hundreds of other chores around the Kokugikan, including errands and services for officials of the association. On tours they go ahead of the wrestlers to put up canvas, haul equipment, and make reservations. They also carry and strike the drum to announce the opening of a basho, and climb the high tower in front of the Kokugikan to beat the drum there at the beginning and end of every tournament day. Yobidashi used to belong individually to the various stables, but they are now united in a quasi-labor union (Yobidashi Kumiai) under the association. Their number is limited to thirty-eight, but there are now only slightly over twenty due to the hard work and small remuneration.

Brief mention should be made of three crucially important behind-the-scenes actors in the sumo drama, the wakamono-gashira, the *sewanin*, and the *tokoyama*. The wakamono-gashira, mentioned in an earlier chapter, belong to stables and are usually retired wrestlers who never got beyond maku-shita but want to remain in the sumo world. They manage the younger wrestlers in divisions below maku-shita, rising early each morning to awaken their charges, supervise them in the keikoba before the oyakata arrive, and teach them sumo etiquette. Their job includes various other tasks around the stable and at the basho, where they supervise the boys fighting in early bouts as well as the wrestlers receiving prizes during the awards ceremony on the last day of the tournament.

The wakamono-gashira are aided by the sewanin (assistants) who are also retired wrestlers of non-sekitori rank. The sewanin serve as equipment and transport managers. Very few heya have both a wakamono-gashira and a sewanin—many have neither one—and the jobs really overlap a great deal.

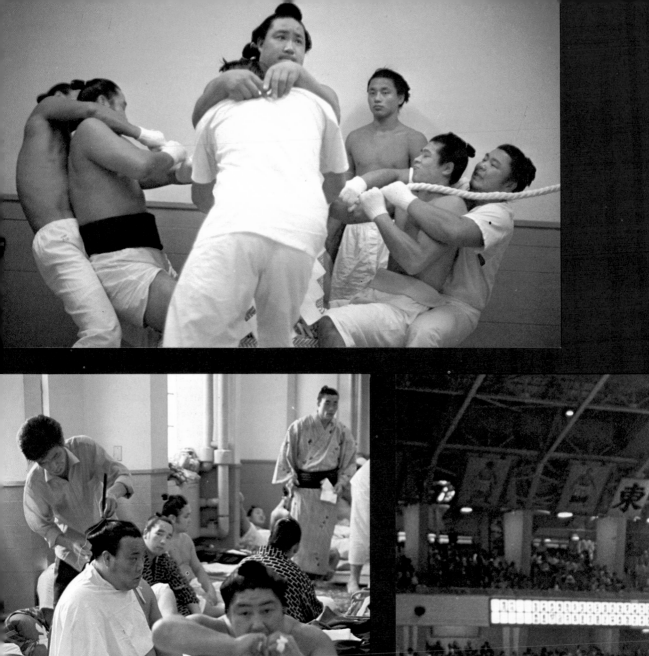

Prior to the commencement of the main bouts of the day—the Maku-uchi division—the hall fills up, and network T.V. takes up the action, while in the dressing-room the wrestlers are having their hair arranged into the chon-mage, and six assistants, in white gloves, help the yokozuna tie on the twenty-five pound tsuna.

Sumotori do not dress their own hair. This job is entrusted to the skilled tokoyama (hairdressers) who make the styling of the chon-mage and oicho-mage a profession. It is said to take between five and eight years to learn how to create the elaborate oicho-mage. Employed at the various stables, these sumo barbers must grease, comb, and pull tight each wrestler's chon-mage every day after practice, and cut, trim, and shave the hair when necessary. They also accompany the sekitori to the dressing room on tournament days to fashion the oicho-mage masterpiece before the bout and return the hair to the normal chon-mage later. A few of the older, larger stables—among them Takasago-beya—are fortunate to have three or four tokoyama, but they are definitely exceptions. Most large heya have only one. The smaller stables have none, and must rely on the stylist of the parent in their ichimon or an unrelated heya nearby. Perhaps the most pervasive smell in any sumo stable is the slightly sweet aroma of the grease used to keep the chonmage in shape. It is a constant reminder that some thirty hairdressers serve the entire body of professional sumotori. Like the yobidashi, the unsung tokoyama are in short supply.

A final element of sumo gishiki is the sad and moving *danpatsu-shiki* (cutting the topknot ceremony), held at Kokugikan during the week after Tokyo tournaments when a sekitori has decided to finally hang up his mawashi. The retiring wrestler sits at ring center in formal kimono and, as he brushes away tears with a handkerchief, his friends, sponsers, and a few fellow wrestlers file solemnly up one by one to cut a tiny lock of his hair with scissors provided by the tate-gyoji. The final cut is made by the sekitori's stablemaster who snips off the entire topknot.

The danpatsu-shiki is included in a day-long program of amusements called *hana-zumo,* a series of songs, comedy, and entertainment that serves to lighten the somber mood of the main event. The proceeds go the retiring wrestler. An exhibition tournament is held and small prizes awarded, although most sumotori do not resist to the bitter end when forced to the edge. To unleash an utchari throw would mean tumbling off the raised dohyo and risking injury. While wrestlers are hardly conscious of the potential danger of falling over this drop in the heat of a tournament struggle, it is foolish to risk it when nothing is at stake.

Among the other attractions at hana-zumo are the resonant voices of the wrestlers as they sing sumo songs (*jinku*) individually and in groups. But the most popular feature is comic sumo (*shokkiri*). Two maku-shita wrestlers go through a hilarious, acrobatic parody of the real thing: missing each other completely at the tachiai, spitting water during the shikiri, sparring like boxers, chasing each other up the aisles and into the audience, sneaking up from the rear to whack the other's head with the water ladle or his back with the yobidashi's broom, and going through a tumbling series of cartwheels and somersaults while locked in the yotsu grips. Then a wrestler takes on a group of tiny boys, all wearing mawashi. The boys rush their giant opponent singly, in groups, and finally all together, their heads crashing into him somewhere around the knee. The

The sad danpatsu-shiki *ceremony. When a* sekitori *wrestler retires, his associates and patrons each solemnly cut off a lock of his hair.*

sumotori spins them around and gently plops them down or out of the ring, but occasionally lets himself be felled.

Hana-zumo is sometimes held purely for charity (*jizen-zumo*) on occasions when there is no danpatsu-shiki. At such times the wrestlers are joined by popular singers, bands, and other entertainers. But the sumotori hold their own. Most wrestlers are excellent singers and not a few are in the professional class. Kitano-fuji made best-selling recordings before becoming a yokozuna, and many are asked to sing at parties and other informal gatherings. I remember taking one of my tsukebito, a young wrestler named Sadamisaki, along with me to a cabaret one night with a group of my patrons. He was asked to take the microphone, and though he hesitated, I made him go ahead. He put the club's vocalists to shame and got so many encores I thought we'd never get home.

Shobu

With all its glitter and solemn, age-old pageantry, the sumo drama comes down in the end to the two men who face each other in the ring. Thinking back over the bouts (*shobu*) I've fought over the years, many stand out: my first appearance as a ranked wrestler in jo-no-kuchi, my first match against a sekitori a little while later, the final win during the basho in which I had to make ten to stay in juryo, or any of the matches during my championship tournament. But one I remember especially vividly was a bout against yokozuna Tamanoumi on the first day of the September Tokyo basho of 1971. I was a komusubi at the time. Fighting a yokozuna is a great thrill for any sekitori and usually brings out his best. This bout in particular, however, has stayed with me perhaps because it illustrates so well what I feel like in the ring, what shobu to me is all about, win or lose. And it has added poignancy due to a regrettable fact I couldn't have known then. It was the last time I would ever fight that powerful yokozuna. Tamanoumi died suddenly the following month at the peak of a potentially great career.

I shall try to recall that day.

In the shitaku-beya muffled conversations and the excited voice of the television announcer describing the bouts interfere with concentration. I sit restlessly in a light cotton kimono, mentally struggling with my opponent in the contest to come, and dividing my gaze between the broadcast from the dohyo only a few hundred feet away and the straw-matted floor in front of me. Wrestlers come and go in silence. Departing faces, grimly determined, are met at the door by the expressions of elation and despair of those returning—their mind already on tomorrow's watch. For me there is still today. My bout is the final one, for I am to take on the supposedly invincible holder of sumo's highest rank, a yokozuna, Tamanoumi. I have fought him before many times. I know him well. He's big, tough, and smart. I think over my past bouts with him, guessing at what he is most likely to do. Will he fight in close trying to secure a migi-yotsu, his speciality, or surprise me with a fast thrusting attack? Should I charge hard using

◀*Overleaf, Takamiyama against yokozuna Tamanoumi; Takamiyama lost the bout despite the apparently certain victory shown here. (see above)*

my weight advantage or sidestep his charge to force him off balance? I wonder what he expects me to do?

I take off my kimono, and my tsukebito begins to wind my heavy silk tournament mawashi around my belly. I can feel sweat breaking out all over my body as little butterflies lay claim to my stomach. I've been here before, countless times, and perhaps my stomach doesn't rise up to my throat the way it used to. But the butterflies never go away. And this is good—it means I'm not overconfident; I'm not going to make any careless mistakes in there. The pounding, rushing sensation in my temples has begun, too, as I itch to be in the ring. That elusive but all-important "fighting spirit" is surging. It's time to leave. I reach the first of three mental peaks of psychological preparation. I'm up. I decide to go all out at the tachiai and force him quickly out of the ring with a relentless pushing and thrusting attack. My tsukebito sponges the sweat from my body and replaces an errant lock of hair, and I can feel the fighting spirit momentarily subside. But as I enter the arena down the hanamichi, and sit down cross-legged on a cushion below the dohyo to await my bout, I can feel it begin to grow again.

Tamanoumi enters through the opposite hanamichi and sits down directly across from me. We cross arms simultaneously, lock eyes, and glare manacingly at each other, oblivious of the two combatants in the ring above us. Psychological warfare has begun. I don't need words to tell him that his size, rank, and ability do not intimidate me, that I'm going to shove him right out of the circle. I search his face for some slight indication of a possible weakness, a lack of concentration, to try to gain the mental upper hand from the outset. Does he turn away and adjust his mawashi to unnerve me or have I really won this preliminary struggle? I'm impatient with time, my mind and body straining toward that one moment when we will crash together and I will throw him out. Today I feel good, strong. I'm ready. Gotta get in there. Gotta win. Now.

As my fighting spirit peaks for a second time, I am jarred by the high-pitched trill of the yobidashi, who stands above me with outstretched fan. "West, Ta—ka—mi—ya—ma." At last, it's time. The yobidashi turns to the east to call my opponent. I rise, slowly, squatting for a moment to flex my legs as my enemy rocks his bulk off his cushion. We ascend the clay mound together.

In separate corners of the dohyo we begin the preliminaries: for the purists, perhaps, a religious ritual, a purification rite, but for me some last limbering-up exercises and, much more, an intensification of the cold war. We first clap our hands to attract the gods. Who will they help this time, I wonder. Then, raising each leg in turn high in the air, we force it down on the dirt with a resounding thud. I feel the dohyo shudder beneath me, and hope that, along with the evil spirits, Tamanoumi quails too. I sense my strength become concentrated as I build toward the last and highest peak.

The gyoji has, in the meantime, joined us and is announcing our names once again. Tossing a handful of salt from a bucket in the corner, I squat down at the edge of the circle, facing my enemy. We clap our hands again in unison,

The yokozuna ceremony marks the beginning of the bouts in the top Maku-uchi division. It is solemn ritual with a religious tradition and, at the same time, demonstrates the strength and nobility of the sekitori.

Above, *a wrestler, sitting on his cushion, waits beside a judge for his bout.* Right, *salt-throwing, part of the purification ritual before each bout.*

Left and right, *young wrestlers in the lower divisions employ* tsuppari (*slapping*).

Left, *both wrestlers have* hidari-yotsu (*left-hand inside on the belt*) *positions.* Right, sukui-nage (*an inside arm throw*).

A wrestler heaves his opponent out of the ring—tsuri-dashi.

Trying for a soto gake (*toppling an opponent by wrapping a leg round from the outside*).
Overleaf, attempting a nodawa (*pushing against the throat*). ▶

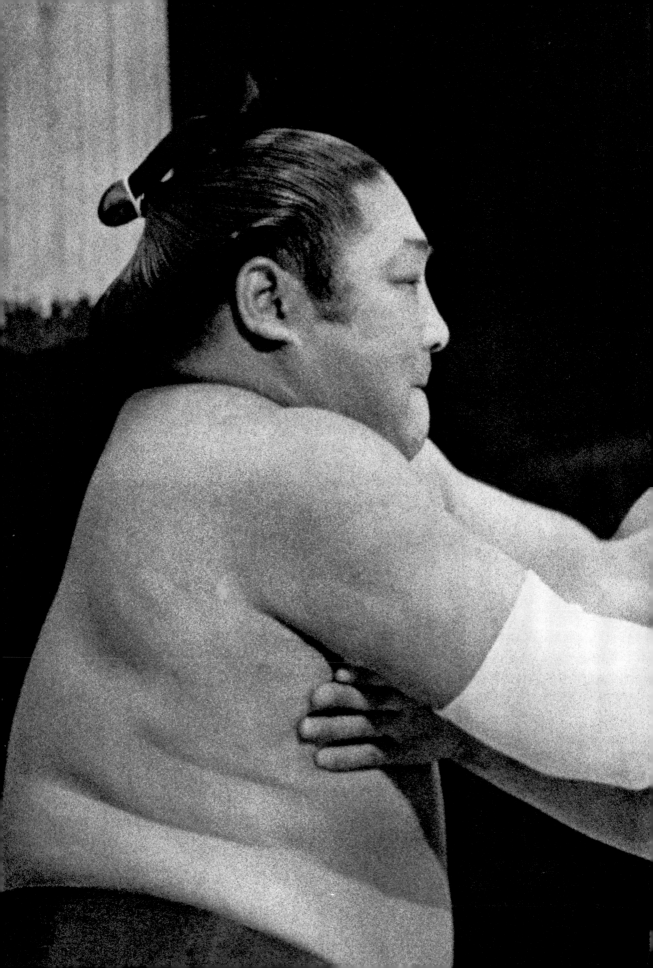

At the end of each tournament day a Maku-shita division wrestler performs the bow ceremony. (See following pages also)

then raise our arms high to the side and rotate the palms to show we are unarmed. As if I needed any weapons today. I glare at my opponent across the ring and play with the idea of sidestepping him at the charge, a tactic I rarely use and one he's surely not preparing for. Rising, we return to our corners for more salt. Then we move to the center of the ring, perform a final shiko, and squat down facing each other to begin the last act in the war of nerves, the shikiri.

I face a mountain: 290 pounds or so of sloping shoulders, protruding belly, and those pillars which are called thighs and legs on ordinary mortals. I can see the ridges of muscle in his belly as he breathes. And he is a yokozuna, invincible, a terrifying psychological advantage which he exploits to the full by gazing at me with the disdain of a man about to crush a cockroach. I glare back. We rise from the squat slowly, leaning down to place both fists on the dirt in front of us, our backs now parallel to the ground. Eyes meet and glower, only inches apart. His neck slung downward, huge mounds of muscle jut from his shoulders. I grind both fists into the sandy surface, looking right through him to that place outside the ring where he will soon, so soon, be thrust in defeat. We lift our fists from the ground, beginning to rise, our eyes brought momentarily even closer together. Almost touching. Fully upright, we continue to glare hard at each other. He turns away first and we go back to our corners for more salt. He's strong on the belt—I have to prevent him from getting his favorite migi-yotsu. But he won't have that much time anyway. Tossing salt in the air, we meet again at the center. Down once more, fists burrowing into the dirt, the silent war intensifying.

We rise again, eyes locked together, but I turn my back in a sudden gesture of contempt. He's mine today. I strain toward the moment when he will know it. My eagerness fights time. Four minutes can't be this long. Head pounding, stomach churning, I grab more salt. Squatting again, sandy fists clenched, beating the dirt. My senses sharpen and I notice detail: droplets of perspiration on his massive belly, the black of his mawashi against his pink skin, the warmth on my shoulders from the spotlights up under the roof. It must be time. Not yet. We glower, rise. I hear the crowd for the first time, a voice calling out my name. But the sounds fade, as does even an awareness of the gyoji only a few feet away. We are alone, performing this deadly ballet only for each other. I ache to pour out my strength, to release the tightly coiled spring my body has become.

The salt corner again, but this time a yobidashi is standing up at the edge holding out a wet towel. The signal. It's time. At last. I scoop out a final handful of salt, hurl it to the heavens, and touch my fingers to my tongue. Back in the center, but this time no fists in the dirt. We bend our knees and lean forward, the gyoji over us flicking his gunbai backward to tell us what we already know. This is it. I crouch down, eyes fixed on my target, abandoning at the last minute any thought of stepping aside. I'll drive into him with everything I've got and send him flying. A huge vein throbs on his kneck. Everything goes suddenly blank. I feel pure force.

Tachiai! We lunge. Collision. I jab a hand at his throat, then his chest. Shock from wrist to elbow. Like straight-arming a boulder. But he's forced back. He counters with a thrust to my chest, but I can barely feel what's sure to ache later. I thrust more quickly. I've got him. We're at the edge. His feet brace against the straw rim. Just one more good push. Overeager to finish him off, I slip slightly bringing our chests crashing together. Recovering, I ram my right hand under his chin. My nodowa forces his body to bend back like a drawn bow. He curls his forearm around my back, desperately trying to steady himself, to stay in the ring. His knees begin to fold. No man can stand this. He must fall, he must. Suddenly, impossibly, he spins to the right. Thrown off balance, I lunge toward defeat. I reach desperately for a grip, any grip, on his belt. He moves further to his right along the straw rim as I try to get my pushing attack restarted. Gotta regain balance. Then I feel his forearm come down on my shoulder like a sledgehammer. Sukui-nage. I gasp—and I'm breathing sand. The crowd roars.

I stagger to my feet, neck throbbing, each breath tearing at my constricted throat. Walking across the ring, I stop to face my conqueror and bow, struggling not to allow the disappointment I'm only beginning to feel show on my face. The blinding lights above, only moments ago so warm, so protective, now nakedly expose, indeed seem to magnify, my defeat before onlooking thousands. I long to be transported away, anywhere that's not here in front of all those people. As Tamanoumi bows to me and squats down to receive the prize money from the gyoji, I step down from the dohyo, pause at the corner to bow once again, then hurry down the endless hanamichi toward the dressing room. I learn later that the bout lasted 2.7 seconds.

Takamiyama rejoices after reading the banzuke *and finding he's reached the Maku-uchi division.*
(Takamiyama's collection)

VII

Okome

"How much bread do you guys make?" "How are you paid?" Everybody seems to want to know. In sumotori slang its called *okome* (rice) from the Tokugawa period days when wrestlers were paid stipends in rice by their feudal patrons.

Unfortunately, there is no simple answer. An amazingly complex system used by the Sumo Association determines salary, allowances, prizes, and fringe benefits. A further complicating factor is that sumotori receive a large amount of gift okome from patrons and others which varies tremendously from wrestler to wrestler and defies calculation. To explain fully even that portion which is calculable would require a separate volume. I will try only to give a general idea of the basic elements of the system and of how almost perversely obstruse it can be. Sometimes I don't even know myself how much I should be getting.

Gekkyu, teate, and hoshokin

Since 1957, sekitori wrestlers have been entitled to a fixed monthly salary (*gekkyu*). To this is added a special monthly allowance (*teate*). Raises have been given periodically, but the figures effective from January 1972, per month, are:

Rank	Gekkyu	Teate	Total
Yokozuna	¥315,000	¥35,000	¥350,000
Ozeki	244,000	30,000	274,000
Sekiwake and			
Komusubi	158,000	25,000	183,000
Maegashira	101,000	20,000	121,000
Juryo	80,000	15,000	95,000

(One U.S. dollar is worth about ¥270.)

The salary is, however, only the starting point. We must also include the special tournament allowance (*basho teate*), expenses for basho outside of Tokyo, and an intricate reward system for winning performances (*hoshokin*). The basho teate is given only to wrestlers in the sport's four highest ranks. It is paid for every tournament, six times a year. Traveling expenses for the three basho in Osaka, Nagoya, and Fukuoka are paid to all sekitori and calculated on the basis of a daily lodging and allowance sum which is multiplied by thirty-five, the number of days provided for. Basho teate and traveling expenses are as follows:

Rank	Basho teate (Six times a year)	Traveling expenses (Three times a year)
Yokozuna	¥200,000	¥210,000
Ozeki	150,000	157,000
Sekiwake and Komusubi	50,000	108,500
Maegashira	None	73,500
Juryo	None	52,500

The way the hoshokin or reward money is determined is probably understood fully only by the poor employees of the association who must sit down and do the figuring. But this money, which applies to all wrestlers from jo-no-kuchi up, is cumulative throughout a sumotori's career. It is paid at every basho, and is an important part of his okome. For some archaic reason, hoshokin is calculated in very small units of yen and *sen* (an old denomination no longer used, 100 sen = 1 yen) and looks like a mere pittance on paper. Fortunately, each unit is multiplied by 1000. Hoshokin is paid every tournament figured on a basic rate by rank:

Rank	Basic hoshokin unit	Actually receive (Basic unit times 1000)
Yokozuna	¥150	¥150,000
Ozeki	100	100,000
Sekiwake, Komusubi and Maegashira	60	60,000
Juryo	40	40,000
Maku-shita and below	3	3,000

These basic units are guaranteed minimums for each rank, but this requires a little explanation. A wrestler's hoshokin is based on winning performances. From the time a sumotori passes out of maezumo and on to the banzuke, he is credited with 50 sen (in reality 500 yen) for every win in a tournament that occurs after he has achieved kachi-koshi (a majority of wins), including the bout which put him over the top. This amount does not differ with rank. For sumotori in maku-shita and below, every victory from and including the fourth one means 500 yen; for those in juryo and above, the 500-yen reward is applied from the eighth win. Thus a sekitori wrestler with an 8–7 record would receive 500 yen, one with a perfect 15–0, 400 yen. Once a 500-yen unit has been won, it is never lost and becomes a permanent part of the wrestler's hoshokin income he receives every tournament. Take a maegashira with a 10–5 record in a basho as an example: his eighth, ninth, and tenth wins would earn him a total of ¥1,500 at that tournament but he will receive far more because this 1500 is added to all the 500-yen units he has earned in each previous basho since his first appearance in jo-no-kuchi. To calculate the amount he will receive in hoshokin for that 10–5 tournament, his career aggregate must be added up. For example, if he has previously had 130 wins above kachi-koshi, he will have received ¥65,000 (130 × 500 yen) at the previous tournament. This time he will get ¥65,000 + ¥1,500 = ¥66,500 in hoshokin and begin the next basho with this new base. There is no penalty. Should be win only five bouts next time around, he will still receive the ¥66,500; should he win nine next time, another ¥1,000 would be added. If a wrestler's career aggregate is less than the basic unit of the division to which he is newly promoted, it will be automatically upped to that division's base upon promotion; if it is more, the basic unit has no meaning for him as he will receive his pay based on the higher amount.

Other units are also added to the aggregate. Maegashira who topple a yokozuna (called receiving a *kinboshi* or gold star) receive a ten-yen unit (thus ¥10,000) which becomes, like the 0.5-yen unit described above, a permanent part of his hoshokin pot every other month. A kinboshi does not, however, depend on making kachi-koshi. If the gold star were a wrestler's only win in that basho, he would still have ¥10,000 added to his total. Similarly, winning the Emperor's Cup adds a 30-yen unit (¥30,000) while an undefeated championship means a 50-yen addition (¥50,000). Thus it is possible for giant-killers and tournament winners to compile better aggregates than some other wrestlers of a higher rank. Through the September basho of 1970, for example, komusubi Hasegawa, who does particularly well against stronger men, compiled ¥158 (¥158,000), and maegashira number eight Wakanami, who had won a previous championship, totaled ¥143 (¥143,000), placing them numbers six and seven respectively in hoshokin take. In contrast, ozeki Maenoyama's total was only ¥104 (¥104,000), although his salary and allowances were of course higher than either Wakanami or Hasegawa. Perhaps the greatest money-winner of all time was yokozuna Taiho. It has been reported that Taiho, who won a record thirty-two championships, some of them undefeated performances, was receiving near the end of his career ¥1,489,000 every basho in hoshokin alone.

Wrestler's below juryo do not actually receive their hoshokin, even though it is recorded. The money is only realized after the wrestler becomes a sekitori at which time he will receive for his first basho in juryo either his aggregate up to that point or the juryo basic hoshokin unit of ¥40, whichever is greater. Sumotori in maku-shita and below do, however, receive a flat fee, not subject to multiplication for victories of two types: any win, regardless of record; and a win that occurs above kachi-koshi, but including the victory that determined it:

Rank	Any single win	Wins from kachi-koshi on
Maku-shita	¥1000	¥3000
Sandanme	600	2000
Jo-nidan and Jo-no-kuchi	400	1500

But these wrestlers only fight seven times a basho and the money, which is not cumulative like hoshokin, is not considerable. For each tournament they do also receive a basho teate as follows:

Rank	Basho teate
Maku-shita	¥25,000
Sandanme	17,000
Jo-nidan	14,000
Jo-no-kuchi	12,000

Other allowances include train fare to and from the tournament site as well as favors and tips from a sekitori or heya support group. There is no fixed salary, or receivable hoshokin unless they make it into juryo. These wrestlers are the living proof of the severity of the sumo world and of the very keen incentives to make sekitori. Money comes to the mighty.

Other minor emoluments are the privileges of the highest ranks. Yokozuna and ozeki receive congratulatory awards of ¥200,000 and ¥100,000 respectively when they achieve those lofty plateaus. Yokozuna are granted as well a ¥100,000 stipend per basho for renewing their ceremonial rope-belt.

One last element in the official income of the sumotori is prize money. Winning a championship in any of the six divisions brings in some okome along with the trophy. The cash prize for winning the Emperor's Cup is ¥1,000,000— this is in addition to the basic unit added to the hoshokin for a championship performance. The reward is less for crowns in the lower divisions. Each of the three prizes up for grabs for wrestlers below the ozeki rank in the maku-uchi division at every basho—the *shukun-sho* (outstanding performance award— given for toppling the most ozeki and yokozuna), *gino-sho* (technique award), and *kanto-sho* (fighting spirit award)—carries with it a ¥200,000 reward. Tournament victors in the highest division also receive a host of other cups and plaques from government, broadcasting, and business organizations, most of which carry a cash award as well.

Finally come the prizes donated by sponsors (*ken-sho*). When the yobidashi walk around the ring before a bout in single file carrying large banners with the names of companies or establishments written on them, okome is involved. Each banner means ¥15,000 and the winner takes all. The victorious wrestler actually receives only ¥10,000, however, the rest being put away to be given at retirement. Most bouts are not sponsored, and ones that are usually have only one or two banners. But the number can approach ten or so for struggles between two very popular sumotori.

Putting a wrestler's official income together to come up with a yearly total is a risky business because of hidden benefits and complex calculations. But to get some idea, we may take a hypothetical sumotori who has gone up and down between komusubi and sekiwake whose aggregate hoshokin is ¥65 (¥65,000), and who has won the shukun-sho and kanto-sho once each during the year. (The hoshokin would of course change from basho to basho if his records were good ones.) His gekkyu and special monthly teate would come to a total of ¥2,196,000 for twelve months. Added to this is ¥300,000 in basho teate, ¥390,000 in hosho-kin, ¥325,500 in traveling allowance, and ¥400,000 for the two prizes for a total of ¥3,611,000, or a little over U.S.$13,000. But even this rough figure is deceptive because it does not include the money from sponsor prizes, gratuities for radio and television appearances, and the all-important okome donated by patrons, incalculable sources which could and often do double or triple his income. Yokozuna and ozeki, of course, make more. Even men at the pinnacle of the sumo pyramid, however, and this includes exceptional bread-winners like the ex-yokozuna Taiho, cannot expect to make much more than half of what top stars in other sports such as baseball and pro-wrestling haul down. For the less successful exponent comparisons with other glamour sports in Japan would probably be even more unfavorable.

Sekitori receive a retirement allowance (*yorokin*) when they decide to hang up their mawashi. Yokozuna receive ¥6,500,000; ozeki ¥5,000,000; sekiwake, komu-subi, and maegashira ¥3,500, 000, and juryo ¥2,500,000. To this basic amount is added an additional allowance per basho, which considerably increases the final total and differs according to rank. It is calculated on the basis of the number of basho the retiring sumotori has been in at each level throughout his career. Yoko-zuna, ozeki, sekiwake, and komusubi qualify for the full retirement benefits of their rank one tournament after promotion. Men retiring at the maegashira or juryo level must have wrestled twenty straight basho or a total of twenty-five basho in their divisions to qualify for the full rewards of their respective ranks, although a single tournament as a komusubi qualifies a wrestler for full maegashira benefits and one as a maegashira for the full juryo earnings. Men who do not qualify are paid a lesser amount, graded in a complex manner on the basis of their career records. Yokozuna and ozeki who are deemed to have contributed greatly to the enhancement of sumo may also receive upon retirement a special "meritorious deeds" award, which is determined by the board of directors of the Sumo Association.

As in the case of salary, non-sekitori wrestlers are left out of the retirement gravy. The only guaranteed pay to men who quit in maku-shita and below is a pitiful severance: at least ¥50,000 for maku-shita, at least ¥30,000 for sandanme, and at least ¥20,000 for jo-nidan and jo-no-kuchi. To qualify for the severance pay, a wrestler must have appeared in fifteen basho or more. These men probably also receive a gratuity from the association for their efforts, but the financial fate of a man who has labored long without reaching juryo is not a happy one.

Tanimachi

The hidden part of the sekitori's income comes largely from his patrons or *tanimachi*. The word is said to derive from the Tanimachi section of Osaka where, at the end of the Meiji period (early twentieth century), there lived a dentist who was such a sumo fan that he gave free treatment to all sumotori.

Support groups and fan clubs for sports and entertainment figures in Japan is common practice, a legacy of the long history of feudal patronage. Sumotori depend heavily on patrons to supplement an income not commensurate with that in more modern sports. One long-time observer pointed out that as long as the benevolence of the tanimachi continues, sumo salaries will rise only gradually.

Tanimachi either back up a wrestler or heya as individuals or form themselves into support groups (*koenkai*). These koenkai exist to encourage and reinforce either the sport as a whole, a stable, or a single sekitori. Two examples of clubs that support sumo in general are the Tamarikai (a reference to the *tamari*, or places near the dohyo where wrestlers and gyoji wait to get in the ring) in Tokyo and the Tozaikai (East-West Club) in Osaka. The membership of the Tozaikai is limited to seventy, and there is an entrance fee of ¥300,000 and annual dues of ¥50,000. Members are required to attend all fifteen days of the annual Osaka basho each March, forming a stately group in traditional formal attire seated near the dohyo. Like the Tamarikai, the Tozaikai exists to promote the sport in all its aspects. It particularly helps those who need it most, the non-sekitori wrestlers, by giving them awards for good records and inviting them to eat and drink with club members.

Nearly every heya has its own koenkai and some, like Takasago-beya, have several. These groups are usually headed by prominent businessmen or politicians and are dedicated to helping, both through material and spiritual incentives, one particular stable to prosper. Fees vary greatly from special memberships in the tens of thousands of yen to regular ones of no more than a few thousand. Members make frequent visits to the heya to watch training or relax with the oyakata and wrestlers. They also invite stablemen to club gatherings. Club members are invited, in turn, to the parties (*oiwai*) held at every heya on the night of the last day of every basho. At these gatherings the koenkai presents cash rewards to both sekitori and non-sekitori wrestlers who have made kachi-koshi. They also often help a new sekitori to buy the accoutrements of his new rank, like the kesho-mawashi, or a retiring one to buy the expensive toshiyori kabu.

Heya koenkai can figure prominently in stable politics as well. When there is more than one oyakata with the stature and influence to be considered as a successor to a retired or deceased stablemaster, the support of the strongest heya koenkai can be the deciding factor. For the ability to keep support money flowing into the heya as well as to attract new benefactors is an important part of the stablemaster's heavy responsibilities. In stables where there is more than one koenkai, it could happen that support would be split between the candidates. In such cases the oyakata with the most influential group behind him would be in the most favorable position.

Unlike the case of the stable koenkai, not all sekitori are blessed with support groups. The wrestlers with the most tanimachi are usually the strongest and most popular ones, but personality and other intangibles play a crucial role along with success. A sekitori's first koenkai is most commonly from his native district where local pride combines with an interest in the sport to spur club formation. The new sekitori may have also become acquainted with certain of an older stable-mate's patrons by accompanying him on outings during his tsukebito days and thus receive a bit of initial help from that quarter. The home-town or home-prefecture support groups often begin getting organized when the local hero is still in maku-shita to insure that financial help is ready on that great day when the newly-promoted sekitori looks around for quick capital to provide him with the necessities of his new rank. As he rises from juryo to maku-uchi and on up the ladder, others, both individually and in groups, will climb on the bandwagon. Winners, quite naturally, attract the largest followings.

A wrestler's tanimachi come from all walks of life, from politicians, business-men and entertainers to local shopkeepers. The reasons why people take up this often expensive hobby are as various as the individuals themselves. Some un-doubtedly enjoy the prestige gained from having a huge, kimono-clad sekitori at gatherings of friends or business acquaintances. Others are attracted to a certain wrestler because of local or family ties or simply because his wrestling style or personality appeals to them. And there are those individuals everywhere who enjoy basking in the reflected glory of stars and famous figures. But the great common denominator is a love of sumo and a keen desire to see it thrive.

Sekitori with many tanimachi and koenkai are constantly on the go. A steady stream of invitations to restaurants, nightclubs, and gatherings pours in from sponsors, and it is often impossible to meet them all and still have the energy left to practice and compete in tournaments. On such occasions, the sekitori usually receives a gift envelope containing either an individual donation or a group col-lection from koenkai members. The benevolence of the tanimachi makes up a substantial part of the income of most sekitori and is one of the fundamental financial underpinnings of sumo society.

I have been very lucky to receive support from individuals and groups in both Hawaii and Japan. My biggest source of support in Japan is a koenkai headed by a man in the shipping business, Ryoichi Sasagawa. The vice-president is Otoshiro Hamada, who heads the Japan-Hawaii Association, a group which sponsors exchanges and good relations between my home state and Japan and which also helps me out personally. The Japan-Hawaii Association has the largest membership of any group supporting me in Japan. I also have other smaller koenkai, such as the Takamiyama Furendokai (Friends of Takamiyama Club), run by restaurateurs in Kyushu, the Takasaki Koenkai, named after the town in Gumma prefecture which is the headquarters for the group's organizer, a fish wholesaler, and others in such towns as Osaka Nagoya and Sapporo. In Hawaii, besides the support I receive from the 442nd Veteran's Club and the Maui Sumo Association, I have several fan clubs, run by friends in the business world or people who knew me from my amateur sumo days on Maui. And outside of the formal groups, I receive encouragement and assistance from many individuals in both Japan and Hawaii. Without all these interested and generous people behind me, I probably would not be a sumo wrestler today.

Much of my free time is spent with supporters, either jawing in a restaurant, or taking part in more formal affairs, such as the opening of a new department store. I usually take along one of my tsukebito, to give them a chance to get out and perhaps share in a patron's largesse. They often come in handy as well. I once took along my highest-ranking tsukebito, a wrestler named Yamatoryu in maku-shita who is a great cook, when I was being entertained at a sukiyaki restau-rant. The waitress stood beside the table seasoning the simmering meat and vegetables to what she thought was perfection before serving us. Yamatoryu took one bite, frowned, and took over the seasoning from the surprised woman. I must admit it tasted far better after he got through.

The organized functions with patrons usually include a *sainkai* or autograph session. But the autograph hounds get more for their money with me than they do from other sekitori. I usually add "Jesse" at the side of the three large char-acters that form "Takamiyama."

Sumotori are really public property. Everywhere I walk in crowded areas I am whacked, patted, pressed, or grabbled at various points to make sure, I sup-pose, that it's genuine flesh bulging beneath my kimono. Schoolboys fight to shake my hand and mothers thrust bawling babes into my arms for that one eternal·click or in the belief that strength can be transmitted through a momen-tary embrace. Although all Japanese are aware of sumo having at least seen it on television, when people encounter me or one of the other larger wrestlers in the flesh for the first time their reaction is disbelief. "*Dekai na!*" ("he's really huge"). My more thoughtful patrons send double the plane fare so that I may use two seats when I have to fly to meet them. Whether I use two seats or one, however, I always wonder why people look anxiously around at me just before takeoff and then smile broadly, as if relieved, once we are airborne.

VIII

Sanyaku

After I settled down in the upper part of the maku-uchi division in the last half of 1968, life in general became easier, less hectic than during my struggling first few years. I was still far from satisfied with my performance in the ring, however. I needed to maintain heavy training schedules to keep up the pace and to perfect belt-grabbing techniques, to improve my yori-kiri, and prevent opponents from employing the throws against which I was still weak. The ranks of ozeki and yokozuna were always hanging there, tauntingly, above me and the only way to give myself the big boost I needed, as I was forever being reminded by my coaches, was keiko, keiko, and more keiko. But I made it into the sanyaku category at komusubi for the Kyushu basho in November 1969, and held that rank more often than not for the next eighteen months, until I was promoted to sekiwake initially for the September Tokyo basho of 1972, the one after my championship performance. And at last I felt comfortable and secure as a sumo wrestler in Japan.

I felt most at home at Takasago-beya. Breaking into sanyaku is the next big step for any wrestler who enters the upper division and my promotion, even though I slid in and out of komusubi, made me the second highest sekitori in the stable after ozeki Maenoyama. I was not only able to eat, but also to truly enjoy all kinds of Japanese food and, at last, I could understand more and more of the nuances in conversation with my stablemates. I had become an active participant in an environment I once had to battle, both in the heya and outside. But there was one very difficult moment.

One of the saddest days of my life was August 17, 1971, when Takasago died of liver trouble. Coach Furiwake succeeded him as the fifth Takasago. Takasago had been a stern but concerned boss who took a precedent-setting gamble to give me my chance in sumo. He was, too, a father figure, perhaps even more to me than to his other deshi because I had to rely so completely upon him at the outset in my strange new home. He knew well what I was going through during my first years, but he knew as well that his obligation to me was not to provide a shoulder to cry on but to bring out the best I had, to make me a sekitori as soon as possible and give me the tools to go as high as I could. He gave me what he knew best, mental and physical strength. Without in the least minimizing the help and support I have received over the years from so many people, it was Takasago who made me what I am today. And the only way I could possibly

repay him was in the ring. Had he lived just one more year, he could have been with me in Nagoya. That would have made my championship complete.

Hawaiian Japanese, Japanese Hawaiian

As the only bilingual member of my profession, I guess it is natural that I often serve as a channel of communication between the world of sumo and the foreigners, especially Americans, who live in or visit Japan. Although not well known in the United States outside of Hawaii, sumo is surprisingly popular among foreigners living in Japan. The number who make the trip to the Kokugikan or one of the arenas in cities outside the capital is increasing with every basho. There is even a pamphlet containing basic information about the sport and a banzuke, both in English, given out at the entrance of the Kokugikan. Many people also visit Takasago-beya to watch practice and ask me questions. I have been surprised again and again to meet non-Japanese children who follow the sport assiduously and know the wrestlers and their ranks in the same detail that their contemporaries living in the U.S. know the names and records of baseball and football stars. One American housewife told me that the only bright spot in her day when she first came to Japan and was having trouble adjusting was the television broadcast of a basho. So many foreign residents wanted to know more about sumo after my championship that the Foreign Correspondents Club in Tokyo held a "Sumo Night" featuring two fast-rising sekiwake, Wajima and Takanohana, and me. The evening included sumo movies, a question-and-answer session, and a meal of chanko-nabe.

I'm usually called on to meet visiting foreigners curious about the sport when I have the time. In November 1971, I took Kitanofuji and Maenoyama to meet the Baltimore Orioles baseball team that was in Kyushu, just as we were fighting there, for a series of goodwill games with Japanese pro teams. Like many others, they all wanted to know what we ate and drank to get so big, and I explained chanko-nabe and the tremendous quantities of beer and saké that some sumotori consume. Not all wrestlers drink, but the legends of great imbibers from the past is endless. The current Takasago-beya record, probably nothing compared to the good old days, was set by a wrestler who is now one of the coaches: fifty-nine quarts of beer at one sitting.

Another interested visitor was heavyweight boxer Muhammad Ali. He visited Japan in the spring of 1972 for a bout against Mac Foster, and I had a hilarious dinner session with him to the delight of an excited crowd. He asked a lot of questions about our food and training in his customarily witty fashion, but what really set him off was hearing about the yokozuna. When I told him it meant grand champion he immediately wanted to fight with one, claiming that if he knocked him out he'd be champ of Japan.

Being an American, my rise in sumo and adjustment to its life-style has been closely watched by the Japanese and made me very well known. My career has also made me popular back home in Hawaii. It seems incredible that the Hawai-

A celebration party in Takasago-beya.

Above, a banquet in Hawaii. From left to right, *Jesse's Mother, Jesse, Takasago (the fourth), Takasago's wife, and coach Furiwake (the present Takasago).* (Takamiyama's collection) Below, *August 1972, opening the Takamiyama Sumo Dohyo on Maui during a visit after the championship tournament.* (Takamiyama's collection)

ian press is actually talking about me when they use expressions like "state hero" and "pride of Maui." I don't know how the hell I got so lucky as to be claimed by two countries, but I'm not complaining. Sometimes people ask me if I'm not at least a bit schizophrenic, but I really do feel at home in both places. I have felt strange, however, in areas of the United States where people don't know what sumo is. A customs official in California once took a look at my size, top-knot, and kimono and decided that I must be some kooky pro wrestler. And he wasn't the only one. A lot of people came up and asked me if I had ever fought guys like Dick the Bruiser or Destroyer Freddie Blassie, and I would have to explain patiently that sumo is a bit different. At that time I felt that I was Japanese, even though I was in my own country. But such times are rare. When I'm in Hawaii or with American friends in Japan, I feel American. And when I'm with other sumotori or Japanese friends, I feel like one of them. It's hard to say which feeling is stronger.

I will, though, probably settle in Japan after I retire. I've met some of the kindest people in the world here who respect what I have done and really accept me as one of them. Besides, I've lived here since I was nineteen and have gotten very used to the way of life. It would be hard to change back again.

Many talk about the trail I have blazed and ask if I think other foreigners will follow me into sumo. Maybe, but it will be difficult. It's not so much the training, which is tough in all sports, but the life-style that has to be accepted until you get used to heya life and the subservience of being a sumo apprentice. When amateur wrestlers at home ask me about the big leagues in Japan, one of their first questions is: "How much do you make?" They are pretty shocked when I tell them about the financial situation of non-sekitori wrestlers. When other sports are offering huge bonuses to attract young athletes, I doubt that many young foreigners would be interested in sumo, even if they could overcome the culture shock. But I think amateur sumo could be exportable, even to areas where there are not large groups of Japanese ancestory as in Hawaii. I would like one day to have the opportunity to take a group of Japanese amateurs to Hawaii and elsewhere to train boys of other cultures.

Yusho and Clipper Takamiyama-go

The high point of my career so far was of course that day in Nagoya when I beat Asahikuni for the championship (*yusho*) and received the Emperor's Cup. On the opening day of the succeeding basho that September in Tokyo, my yusho picture was hoisted into the rafters of the Kokugikan to join those of other tournament winners of the past few years. Not everyone in the sumo world, however, looked up at my face with pleasure. For sumo's closed and inbred society deeply fears any challenge to the sport's carefully preserved tradition, to its unique Japaneseness. To some, the tournament victory by a foreigner posed just such a threat to sumo's integrity.

During my winning performance, Japan's major sports dailies devoted column

Returning to Hawaii in triumph. (Takamiyama's collection)

after column to background stories on me, and quoted scores of experts and lay-men on their reactions to my possible victory. My hard charge and violent thrusting technique earned me such nicknames as "bulldozer," "dumpcar," and "typhoon." After the ninth day of the basho, when I had sole possession of the lead with an 8–1 record, one oyakata moaned that Japan was about to be humili-ated again. She had lost the gold medal in judo's unlimited division to a Dutchman at the Tokyo Olympics in 1964 and it now looked like the nation's national sport itself was about to be taken over by a foreigner. Three days later, with me still out in front at 10–2, one sports newspaper headlined: "National Sport in Danger! Stop Jesse!" Certain officials wondered, only half in jest, if they should substitute the Star Spangled Banner for the Japanese national anthem at the awards cere-mony should I win. Purists argued with internationalists over whether sumotori from other countries were good for the sport. When victory was assured with my thirteenth win on the final day, one sumo critic angrily commented: "This is no joke. Can we call this our national sport? Despite his weak points, there were only two Japanese wrestlers who could manage to beat Takamiyama. I guess we can't brag much about our national sport anymore."

Happily, such voices were definitely minority ones, and in many cases I think were the outpouring of frustration over the lackluster performances of the top-ranked yokozuna and ozeki in the immediately preceding tournaments. Far more common were the echoes of praise and respect, making it downright embarrassing for me to open the paper. The president of the Sumo Association pointed out that while the loss in judo was to a man trained in his own country, my victory was the hard-earned product of long years in Japan under Japanese coaches. Sports columnists stressed what they called my astounding amount of training and fur-ther flattered me by noting that many Japanese wrestlers who were slacking off could learn a great deal from my example. And the average fan's reaction really made me feel at home. Typical were the remarks of a company president from Nagoya: "He struggled for over eight years in a strange land. I'm, frankly, hap-py as hell he won. He's not American anymore, he's Japanese." But the com-ments of one of sumo's leading television commentators, ex-wrestler Shoichi Kamikaze, made me the most proud: "The notion that the national sport of sumo cannot be lost to a foreigner is an odd one. Takamiyama came to Japan nine years ago and put out more than twice as hard as other wrestlers. He's not a foreigner. He's a sumo wrestler of Japan."

The storm of words was followed by a barrage of phone calls. I've never been so busy in my life. All of a sudden people I'd never heard of wanted to meet me and get me to do something, from selling products and appearing on television to visiting their store. While I'd been used to public attention for some time, instant stardom was something else, fun for the first few days and then a bit too much. I finally told my tsukebito at the heya to tell everyone I was out, or in the bath, anything. Just making the rounds of my friends and patrons left little time for sleep. I was even received by Prime Minister Kakuei Tanaka and had a

Above, *Takamiyama with Muhammad Ali in Japan.* (Baseball Magazine). Above right, *Takasago-beya wrestlers carry a portable shrine through the streets of Tokyo.* (Takamiyama's collection)

Right, *Reading the sumo report the morning after.* (Takamiyama's collection)

good laugh comparing hand sizes with him. And all the while the people back home were clamoring for my return as soon as possible. My crowded schedule in Japan both before and after I returned briefly to Hawaii to be honored there, left little time for training and was perhaps largely responsible for my poor 5–10 performance in the following September basho.

Though I'd been home several times since my first return in 1966, and always received warm, excited welcomes, my three-day trip in August, 1972 was beyond my wildest expectations. The party accompanying me included my old stable-master's wife, the present Takasago and his wife, my friend and mentor Otoshiro Hamada, my senior tsukebito Yamatoryu, and hairdresser Takaju Hinahata. The Pan Am clipper we used to make the trip over was renamed for the voyage "Clipper Takamiyama-go" ("go" means number or issue in Japanese) in large letters painted on the side of the aircraft. The day of my arrival in Honolulu, August 23, was officially proclaimed "Takamiyama Day" by the governor, and I found myself in the rather unique position of being a state guest in my home state for the entire brief visit. After a huge welcome at the airport and a motor-cade to the State Capitol, I was officially welcomed home by Governor John Burns who presented me with gifts. That night I was treated to a gala cocktail party and reception. Throughout the three days, which included trips to Maui and the big island of Hawaii, Lieutenant Governor George Ariyoshi never left my side, even when the celebrations continued into the wee hours of the morning.

The return to Maui on the 24th showed that the hometown folks were not going to be outdone by the officials in Honolulu. I was given a huge airport recep-tion upon arrival and that night attended a massive luau in my honor. The high-light of the day was dedicating a new practice ring for the Maui Sumo Club named after me: the Takamiyama Sumo Dohyo. It is situated in Maui's war memorial complex just below my alma mater, Baldwin High School. After the ceremonies, I put on my mawashi and got in the ring against childhood friends and young amateur hopefuls. The next day I left Maui to hop over to Hawaii for a brief visit before returning to Honolulu to prepare for the flight back to Japan. It was a short, hectic, but exhilirating three days, and everywhere I went people told me that they expected my next return to be as an ozeki. I hope they're right.

Epilogue

Nagoya, July 16, 1972—Evening

In the dressing room, I quickly change into formal kimono and walk out of the building through a gauntlet of clapping, screaming fans. I get into the open car, flanked in the back seat by fellow maku-uchi stablemates Maenoyama and Fujizakura, Fujizakura holding high the championship flag. Then we begin a slow parade through the streets of the city back to the heya's temporary quarters. People jam the sidewalks and crowd the windowsills of tall buildings to wave and cheer. I feel my whole face break into laughter and flash the victory sign to everyone. It takes a long time to cover the few short miles, but I have become oblivious to time until we finally pull up in front of the temple.

I jump out and fight my way through the gate as fans and newsmen crowd around. Inside I am greeted by a reception committee of the new Takasago, his wife, the other oyakata, good friends, and patrons. But I make first for a small, elegant lady in kimono and impetuously sweep her up into my arms. The window of the man with whom I most wanted to share this moment plants a tiny kiss on my huge cheek. At first there are no words. Then, sobbing, she gives expression to what everyone gathered there must have been thinking: "If he'd only lived one more year... But I know that, somewhere, he can see the joy on Jesse's face."

I set her gently down and proceed to open a huge barrel of saké with the new Takasago. The stablemaster gives me a toast—the first of what is sure to be an endless number. The initial ceremonies concluded, we head for the large Buddha hall where many friends and supporters have already gathered to join in the merriment, eating, drinking, and speechmaking that will continue far into the night. As I climb the steps of the building, pausing frequently to accommodate the photographers, memories pass suddenly through my mind. The night in Honolulu when I was invited to Japan, the promise to my mother to make good, the many times Takasago's strictness had forced me to tears and thoughts of escaping. Then, reaching my place at the head table to take the first swill of saké from the huge silver victory bowl, I recall my former boss's oft-repeated words: "There's no one more like a sekitori than Jesse, no one more like a Japanese."

Friends and patrons surround the new champion, who sits holding the Emperor's Cup, for the traditional shouts of "Banzai!" (Baseball Magazine)

Index

The macrons over certain vowels indicate that the sound is long